Wars That Changed the World

Wars That Changed the World

Lessons Beyond the Battlefield
(From strategy and politics to innovation and psychology)

Alexander Carter Grey

Mindful Pages

Published in 2025

ISBN: 9789371772440 (PB)
ISBN: 9789371775441 (eBook)

Published by

Mindful Pages
Imprint of Alpha Editions LLC
312 W. 2nd St #1834
Casper, WY 82601, USA

This book was developed using advanced writing tools to support the drafting and ideation process. All content has been thoughtfully curated, refined, and reviewed to ensure quality and relevance.

Content

Introduction
Not Just War: Reclaiming the Hidden Currents of Conflict

History, as it is so often told, flattens war into a timeline—dates neatly marked, battles plotted on maps, alliances traced like lines on a chessboard. Schoolroom charts and national commemorations linger on the visible and the countable: troop movements, tactical gambits, the swelling and ebbing of empires, the treaties that tie off a chapter. These are the spectacles of war—the marching columns, the smoke and steel, the pivots of geopolitics. Yet the truest, most enduring effects of war often reside elsewhere, in places not so easily tallied: in the unseen ruptures of mind and society, in the subtle reorganising—or sometimes the unexpected quickening—of human life.

This is not a book about retelling the well-worn arcs of military glory or moral adjudication, nor about deciding, from a safe temporal distance, who stood on the right side of history. Those narratives have been spun and respun until they gleam. Instead, *Wars That Changed the World* begins where such accounts fall silent: in the quiet after the last gunshot, when the visible theatre closes and something more elusive begins to take shape. It is a study of aftershocks—the tremors in culture, identity, invention—that ripple on long after the armies have gone. Here, war is not merely a clash of arms, but a catalyst, a rewriter of civilisations as much as a destroyer.

Perhaps war is not only rupture, but reflection—a distorted mirror held up to civilisation itself. For all its atrocities, it has also served as one of humanity's most revealing laboratories. When the structures we trust disintegrate, what holds and what gives way becomes startlingly clear. In the breach, moral lines are redrawn; loyalties shift; technologies leap forward at a pace peacetime rarely compels. And we see how, stripped of rules, individuals must renegotiate not only their physical survival but their very sense of self.

Seen in this light, war becomes an amplifier of the human condition. It exposes how nations imagine themselves, how ideologies harden or dissolve, how power is sought, feared, abused, or misunderstood. It presses leadership into sharper relief, revealing the fragility of reason under duress. And it thrusts ordinary people—soldiers, civilians, children—into moments where the choice between action and inaction carries profound moral weight. Whether in the sodden trenches of Flanders, the humming secrecy of Bletchley Park, the scorched aftermath of Hiroshima, or the tentative reconciliations of post-genocide Rwanda, one finds not only devastation but ingenuity, endurance, and moments of piercing ethical clarity.

The argument at the heart of this work is that war must be understood not just as a political or military upheaval, but as a psychological and cultural force—one that rearranges the inner architecture of those who endure it, often leaving deeper traces in memory than in the official record. Peace does not close the ledger. Conflict seeps into stories, myths, classrooms, policies, even the unspoken habits of thought that guide our moral lives. To examine war properly is to study these echoes.

Across ten chapters, we follow these reverberations in their many guises. The journey begins with the human mind. The first chapter ventures into the mental landscape of conflict, asking not merely what war does to flesh and bone, but to the soul. Concepts such as moral injury—the anguish of betraying one's own ethical compass—are explored in both soldiers and civilians caught in impossible dilemmas. Here lie paradoxes: war can shatter thought, yet also ignite sudden clarity or ingenuity. Some even find themselves empathising with the enemy, their battlefield becoming a crucible for unexpected transformation.

Next, we confront the illusions of control that dominate the war rooms of history. Beneath the language of reasoned strategy lies a tangle of fear, impulse, and improvisation. The masterstrokes we admire in hindsight were often desperate wagers. Paranoia becomes policy. Perceptions are crafted and manipulated. The tidy theories of 'rational actors' collapse under the weight of events.

From there, we turn to innovation—the unforeseen offspring of desperation. Some of the modern world's most transformative breakthroughs, from penicillin to the internet, owe their genesis to wartime urgency rather than peacetime planning. War destroys, yes—but it also clears ground for invention. We trace this uneasy duality, technological and psychological alike.

Yet invention is only one thread. This book places civilian life—so often peripheral in martial histories—at its centre. How do communities persist under occupation? How does a culture resist erasure? What becomes of gender roles when entire generations of men are absent? War, like an earthquake, shifts the social terrain: women step into roles denied them before, young people inherit responsibilities far beyond their years, marginalised groups forge new identities. Schools are rebuilt with altered curricula. Resistance movements take root. Art becomes both memorial and defiance.

Then comes the aftermath—not as epilogue, but as a new beginning fraught with struggle. Post-war life demands battles for memory, justice, moral reconstruction. Processes of transitional justice, national reconciliation, and the ethics of remembrance become as critical as any treaty. The way a conflict is remembered—or misremembered—can shape whether the next one ignites.

Some of the most sobering pages turn to children. When the young are drawn into war—not only as bystanders, but as fighters, indoctrinated pupils, or traumatised survivors—their futures, and often their societies', are reshaped for decades. And yet, some of these same children emerge as advocates for peace, bearers of testimony, or visionaries intent on remaking what was broken.

The later chapters look squarely at civilisation itself. War, with its ruptures, uncovers the collective unconscious: our ancient appetite for apocalyptic drama, the chilling bureaucracy of cruelty, the way inner fears are projected outward onto imagined foes. These patterns, hauntingly familiar, thread through millennia—from Homeric epics to the rubble of Aleppo.

Toward the close, the question arises: can the hard-won wisdom of wartime be carried into peacetime? Could the strategic patience of guerrilla fighters inform crisis management in boardrooms or households? Might the moral clarity found in moments of mortal peril guide us through the subtler, slower dilemmas of modern life?

Could empathy, sharpened in the midst of conflict, serve as a tool for building bridges rather than securing battlefields?

We end in the present day, an age in which war often arrives unannounced. Its tools—psychological pressure, economic leverage, cultural erasure—slip easily across borders and screens. These are the newer frontlines, and they require us to recognise the creeping spread of warlike habits into our language, our politics, our technologies, and our own inner worlds.

This book offers neither romance nor naïve pacifism. It is, instead, an invitation to see war differently—to read it not solely through its wreckage, but through what it discloses about ourselves. To consider it not as an external eruption, but as a human constant whose causes and consequences implicate us all.

If we are to imagine a future that is more awake, more steadfast, more just, we must examine not only what war destroys, but what it illuminates. The task here is to recover that hidden knowledge: to learn from war's severest lessons without succumbing to its seductions; to trace the transformations it leaves behind rather than merely reciting its chronicles.

This is not a history of battles. It is a study of what remains—in minds, in social structures, in the silent gaps between memory and meaning. And it asks to be read with the full curiosity of a human being seeking to understand not only what we have been, but what we might yet become.

Chapter 1
The Psychology of the Unthinkable: What War Does to the Human Mind

There is a strange quiet that follows war—not the formal hush of ceasefire agreements nor the strategic pause of demilitarisation, but a deeper, more private silence. It is the stillness that settles over the minds of those struggling to reconcile the world they return to with the one they have just survived. For soldiers and civilians alike, "normal" life can feel strangely discordant, a jarring counterpoint to the chaos that came before. This chapter begins not with the question of what happened, but with the more uncomfortable inquiry: what has it done to those who endured it?

War does more than destroy. It remakes people—often in ways invisible to the eye. The transformation is not only physical, but psychological, existential, neurological. It alters how one thinks, remembers, judges, trusts, and even who one believes oneself to be. Public discussion tends to orbit around post-traumatic stress disorder (PTSD), as if it were the sole psychological legacy of war. Yet PTSD is but one thread in a far more intricate weave. It suggests that the injury comes from without—a horror inflicted upon the self. But some of the most enduring wounds are inflicted from within: moments of moral compromise, personal failure, or perceived cowardice that fracture the ethical framework by which one has lived. This is the terrain of moral injury.

Though the terminology is modern, the phenomenon is ancient. One might argue that Homer's Achilles—haunted as much by guilt as by grief—is among the earliest literary portrayals of it. Today, the term refers to the psychic distress that stems not from being harmed, but from harming—or from witnessing harm and being powerless to stop it. A soldier who mistakenly kills a civilian; a medic unable to save a dying child; a drone operator watching death unfold through a screen—none may be physically touched, yet the damage can be profound and lasting. Moral injury is insidious, eroding from within. It is not about what was done to me, but what I did—or failed to do.

It is a collapse of one's moral architecture, a fracture in the self-story that once lent life coherence.

Unlike PTSD, which often arises from fear-based trauma, moral injury feeds on guilt, shame, and spiritual conflict. It rarely yields to medication. Its treatment lies instead in existential labour: reconstructing a sense of self after an ethical collapse. Some find relief in activism, confession, or storytelling; others sink into isolation, depression, or, tragically, suicide. Its trajectory is unpredictable, yet unmistakable among soldiers, aid workers, and war correspondents who have stood by in the face of preventable suffering. The paradox is sharp: the body comes home, but the conscience remains in the field.

The mind's injuries are not purely moral—they are also neurological. Extreme stress reshapes the brain's chemistry, sometimes permanently. In battle, the mind sacrifices deliberation for instinct. The prefrontal cortex—the centre of reason and moral judgement—often yields to the amygdala's blunt imperatives of fight or flight. Perception narrows. Time distorts. Many soldiers report disassociation, hyper-sensitive hearing, or even synaesthetic crossovers of sense. First World War diaries describe hallucinations, prophetic dreams, and what one British officer called "the feeling of already being dead." These are not flourishes of language; they are the signs of a nervous system stretched to its outer limits.

Yet such strain does not always end in collapse. In some, it triggers startling adaptation. Wartime has produced moments of brilliance in the midst of horror—quick thinking and innovation under pressures that would crush most minds. Prisoners of war in Vietnam devised elaborate communication systems by tapping codes through walls; some created entire imaginary schools or composed symphonies in their heads. One POW, visualising golf swings in obsessive detail, emerged to play the best round of his life. Neuroscience tells us that in such conditions, the brain can rewire itself on the fly. Crisis compresses thought, forcing swift resolution, and—rarely—unlocking forms of problem-solving inaccessible in calmer times.

The psychological history of war is marked by this duality: breakdown and adaptation, collapse and ingenuity. Minds can shatter; they can also sharpen. And sometimes that sharpened clarity takes an unexpected shape: empathy for the enemy.

It is among the strangest—and most disruptive—phenomena in combat. Soldiers have been known to spare foes at the last moment, even at their own peril. The Christmas Truce of 1914 saw Germans and Britons exchanging cigarettes, playing football, and burying the dead together. More isolated accounts tell of fighters freezing when meeting an enemy's gaze, recognising—just for an instant—a reflection of themselves. One American sniper in Iraq described the shock of seeing his own humanity in the man he was about to kill. Such moments pierce the psychological armour of war, which depends on "othering" the enemy. Lift that veil, and the machinery falters. Empathy, far from being a luxury, becomes a dangerous interruption.

These breaches of perspective provoke hard questions: Who, exactly, is the enemy? How fixed is identity under duress? Can the "us" and "them" distinction survive close contact with reality? These questions are not philosophical indulgences—they influence battlefield choices, veterans' mental health, and the narratives nations tell themselves. Some who have spared lives carry guilt; others who have killed without feeling are haunted more deeply. The moral accounting of war is a ledger without balance.

Yet in the rubble of these contradictions, some find a rare form of clarity. War burns away the excess. For some, that reduction is devastating; for others, it distils purpose. Memoirs such as Viktor Frankl's *Man's Search for Meaning* or Marcus Luttrell's *Lone Survivor* are more than survival stories—they are philosophical meditations born of extremity. In the compressed theatre of danger, people sometimes discover what they value most, who they love, what they fear, and what they are prepared to lose. War becomes, in its strange way, an experiment in selfhood.

This transformation is not always a rescue. It can reveal a self one cannot live with, or forge a self that cannot live among civilians. Either way, the battlefield becomes a crucible: burning away illusion, forcing moral choices, revealing character. That is why war literature so often carries existential weight—it reflects the fact that in confronting death, we are also confronted with life, distilled to its sharpest point.

This chapter is neither diagnosis nor elegy. It seeks neither to pathologise nor romanticise the mental states of those who endure war. Rather, it is an unflinching look at what war does to the mind's architecture. We will move between clinical research and personal testimony, from the trenches of history to the imaging labs of modern neuroscience. We will examine how trauma embeds itself in memory, how morality bends or breaks, how empathy can both corrode and redeem, and how devastation can, for some, lead to a reassembled self.

To speak only of strategy, politics, or technology is to miss war's most lasting legacy. Battles end. Armistices are signed. But the wounds carved into memory, morality, and meaning often remain. What follows is an attempt to map the unspoken territory: the psychological aftermath of war, not as an illness, but as a record—etched deeply into the human mind—of the unthinkable made real.

The Paradox of Moral Injury

In war, the human body is not the only thing that bleeds. For some, the deepest wounds are inflicted not by shrapnel or fire, but by actions that rupture the moral frameworks they once held sacred. These injuries are invisible, yet profoundly destabilising. They do not respond to stitches or surgery, and no medal or honour can reconcile them. The term *moral injury*, once marginal in psychological discourse, now demands central attention—not only for what it reveals about combat, but for what it uncovers about the fragile architecture of conscience itself.

Moral injury refers to the internal suffering that arises when individuals perpetrate, witness, or fail to prevent acts that violate their core ethical beliefs. It is not reducible to fear, helplessness, or horror—though those are often present. Rather, it is the psychic dislocation that occurs when one's own actions (or inactions) stand in direct contradiction to deeply held values. Unlike post-traumatic stress disorder, which is rooted primarily in fear-based trauma, moral injury originates from *moral dissonance*: a collapse in the alignment between who one believes oneself to be and what one has done—or been forced to endure.

For many veterans, this fracture remains long after the battlefield has faded. A soldier might return from a deployment with their body intact and their career decorated, only to be tormented by the memory of having followed an order that resulted in civilian deaths, or having hesitated a moment too long at a checkpoint. The guilt does not rest on the legality of the action, nor on public condemnation, but on private reckoning. One Marine described it as "a sickness of the soul," and in doing so captured what formal diagnostics often miss: moral injury is not a psychological disorder. It is a spiritual rupture.

This distinction matters. For years, much of military mental health infrastructure has focused—understandably—on PTSD. Yet clinicians and ethicists alike have begun to argue that PTSD, while often co-occurring with moral injury, cannot fully account for the phenomena reported by many returning soldiers. PTSD responds, at least partially, to exposure therapy and pharmacological treatment. Moral injury often does not. One may manage the panic attacks, regulate the nightmares, and still lie awake at night replaying a single moment in which they acted against their better judgement—or failed to act at all. The healing required is not just psychological. It is moral and relational, involving forgiveness, restitution, meaning-making, and sometimes spiritual transformation.

The roots of the concept can be traced to ancient thought, though its formal articulation is relatively recent. Military psychiatrist Jonathan Shay was among the first to popularise the term in the 1990s, drawing on both Homeric epics and his work with Vietnam veterans. Shay noted that what destroyed many of these men was not combat per se, but betrayal—by commanders, by institutions, or by the self. In his seminal work *Achilles in Vietnam*, he wrote of the soldier's "loss of the capacity for social trust." This loss, he argued, is not a symptom but a scar—a wound to the moral fabric that binds human beings to one another.

Consider the case of British soldiers in the Troubles-era Northern Ireland, who were deployed into a civilian environment rife with political ambiguity. Many were young and unprepared for the complex rules of engagement they would face. The line between combatant and civilian was often blurred, and snap decisions had lifelong consequences. One former soldier described how, decades later, it wasn't the firefights that haunted him—it was the face of an unarmed teenager he had detained with excessive force, suspecting him of carrying explosives. The boy had nothing. No formal complaint was filed. But the image stayed with him, becoming a silent accusation lodged within his conscience. This is the architecture of moral injury: not always catastrophic, not always visible, but internally ruinous.

Civilian populations are not immune. In contemporary conflicts, where warfare is often urban and asymmetrical, civilians are frequently thrust into situations where survival itself becomes ethically compromising. Syrian doctors, for instance, have been forced to triage not only on medical urgency, but on sectarian identity—knowing that saving one patient might invite lethal retaliation. Aid workers in famine zones, tasked with distributing scarce resources, live with the daily knowledge that every decision carries mortal consequences. These individuals, though not combatants, often exhibit the same markers of moral injury: guilt, shame, isolation, and a shattered sense of moral coherence.

At the heart of moral injury lies a paradox: the very capacity for moral reasoning—the ability to recognise right from wrong—is what makes the injury possible. A sociopath cannot suffer moral injury. Only those with a functioning conscience can. This makes moral injury a mark not of deficiency, but of moral depth. It is, in a sense, the shadow side of our ethical awareness. To experience it is to affirm that one's values are not simply performative but integral to identity. And yet, this affirmation comes at a staggering cost.

The persistence of moral injury raises uncomfortable questions. Can one truly be moral in a context designed to override individual ethics? To what extent is responsibility personal in systems of distributed authority, such as militaries or bureaucracies? And what does recovery look like when the harm is not just experienced, but enacted? Traditional models of healing—seeking therapy, taking medication, receiving social support—are often inadequate. What many morally injured individuals seek is something more elusive: moral repair.

Moral repair is not merely the absence of pain. It involves the reconstitution of self in a way that allows for the acknowledgment of wrongdoing without complete moral self-annihilation. This is extraordinarily difficult. It may involve confession, restitution, symbolic acts, or simply the slow, painstaking work of integrating the experience into a revised ethical self-understanding. In some cases, it requires a communal response. Societies that ask individuals to carry out acts in their name must also be willing to hear their stories, to bear witness to their pain, and, where possible, to shoulder part of the moral weight.

There are, to be sure, those who argue that war necessarily involves moral compromise, and that trying to judge it by peacetime ethics is misguided. This perspective, while pragmatic, risks a kind of ethical numbing. The danger lies not in recognising that war is ethically complex, but in surrendering to the idea that it is ethically vacant. Moral injury, when acknowledged and supported, can serve as a counterweight to such cynicism. It reminds us that even in contexts of systemic violence, individuals remain moral agents—and that their suffering is not a weakness, but a sign of retained humanity.

The implications of moral injury extend beyond the battlefield. As societies confront new forms of remote warfare—drones, cyber-attacks, algorithmic targeting—the moral distance between decision and consequence grows. But the injury, when it arrives, is no less real. Drone pilots have reported emotional breakdowns after witnessing the delayed consequences of their strikes. Analysts monitoring digital surveillance feeds have described feeling complicit in violence they never physically participated in. Technology has changed the mechanics of warfare, but not its ethical weight.

There is, too, a growing recognition that the conditions giving rise to moral injury exist in civilian professions. Healthcare workers during the COVID-19 pandemic, for example, faced impossible choices about which patients to prioritise for ventilators. Some later reported symptoms resembling those of combat veterans: guilt, moral disorientation, spiritual numbness. The concept of moral injury, though born in the context of war, is proving broader in application—relevant wherever people are asked to act in ways that violate their moral compass in service of institutional survival.

What then is to be done? First, moral injury must be recognised for what it is: not a fringe phenomenon, but a core component of human response to ethical violation under pressure. It requires its own frameworks of understanding, distinct from but often intersecting with trauma. Second, those who suffer from it must not be pathologised or dismissed as overly sensitive. Their suffering is a measure of their moral integrity. And third, institutions—militaries, governments, healthcare systems—must reckon with the moral burdens they delegate. A society that demands sacrifice must also be prepared to offer moral support, not just therapeutic resources.

If war is the theatre of the unthinkable, then moral injury is the echo that lingers when the curtain falls. It is a quiet, enduring protest from within the self—a refusal to let atrocity become normal, to let conscience be reduced to compliance. In acknowledging its existence, we honour not only those who suffer from it, but the moral foundations they carry, however broken. Moral injury is not a sign of weakness. It is a painful, haunting testament to the human capacity for ethical life—even in the most inhuman of conditions.

Cognitive Collapse and Evolution in Crisis

War does not merely test the limits of physical endurance; it rewires the very machinery of thought. When survival becomes the only metric that matters, the brain begins to adapt—not always in ways that promote accuracy, rationality, or even coherence. The experience of war, particularly under sustained extreme stress, reveals the astonishing plasticity and vulnerability of the human mind. It can unravel perception, fracture memory, distort time, and undermine judgment. Yet paradoxically, it can also produce moments of unanticipated brilliance, creative problem-solving, and new forms of cognition forged in the crucible of crisis. Understanding this duality—collapse and evolution—is critical not only to grasp the inner life of those who endure war, but to appreciate the broader implications for decision-making, resilience, and adaptation under pressure.

Combat stress is unlike ordinary psychological strain. It is not simply a matter of pressure, but of *unrelenting threat*, often combined with uncertainty, deprivation, and moral ambiguity. In such conditions, the brain's primary priority shifts from abstract reasoning to immediate survival. The prefrontal cortex—the region responsible for executive functions like planning, deliberation, and impulse control—takes a secondary role to the limbic system, particularly the amygdala, which processes fear and threat. This neurobiological shift has profound consequences. Soldiers in active conflict zones often report perceptual narrowing: a tunnelled awareness where peripheral details vanish, sound becomes either hyper-accentuated or eerily distant, and time stretches or collapses in unpredictable ways. These are not poetic distortions—they are direct consequences of cortisol and adrenaline flooding the system.

Consider the first-hand accounts from soldiers in the trenches of the First World War. Diaries from the Western Front describe time as "syrupy," as if minutes turned to hours during bombardments, then evaporated entirely in moments of action. One British infantryman, writing during the Battle of the Somme, recalled being unable to hear his own shouting amidst shellfire, while simultaneously detecting the faint scratch of a rat behind him—auditory hypervigilance operating alongside functional deafness. Such cognitive fragmentation reflects the brain's desperate attempt to prioritise threats and conserve processing power. In extreme situations, memory encoding may fail altogether, leading to lacunae—missing hours, even days, as if consciousness itself had selectively erased unbearable segments of reality.

But cognitive collapse is only one side of the story. Just as stress can dismantle ordinary patterns of thinking, it can also provoke radical adaptation. In certain individuals, the same neurological conditions that produce disorientation and dysfunction also produce astonishing mental feats. These may take the form of improvised tactical decisions, novel coping mechanisms, or profound existential insight. Vietnam War POWs, for instance, developed complex communication systems using coded taps and subtle signals, enabling sustained resistance and communal coherence despite years of solitary confinement. One of the most notable cases is that of Admiral James Stockdale, who survived over seven years of captivity by mentally structuring his day into rigorous philosophical reflection, drawing on the Stoicism of Epictetus. For Stockdale, mental discipline became both armour and compass—a way not only to endure, but to grow.

This tension between disintegration and ingenuity has become a focus of neuroscientific inquiry. Studies in the past two decades have explored how acute stress triggers neuroplasticity—the brain's capacity to rewire itself under changing conditions. While chronic stress often damages the hippocampus, impairing memory, it can also lead to increased connectivity in other regions, particularly those involved in motor planning and rapid response. Functional MRI scans of combat veterans show divergent patterns: some exhibit diminished capacity for reflection and empathy, while others demonstrate enhanced responsiveness and pattern recognition. The variables are complex, including personality, training, belief systems, and context. What is clear, however, is that crisis alters cognition—and not uniformly.

Perhaps one of the most illuminating contrasts emerges between structured military training and raw, unmediated experience. Training seeks to automate responses, to instil drills that bypass deliberation. This has undeniable benefits in high-stakes combat, where hesitation can be fatal. But it also creates a cognitive rigidity that can falter under unpredictable conditions. In contrast, untrained civilians caught in conflict zones often develop improvisational skills—what some researchers term *adaptive cognition.* During the siege of Sarajevo, for instance, civilians devised ingenious systems for obtaining water, navigating sniper zones, and maintaining psychological cohesion in the absence of formal leadership. What emerged was not merely survival, but a form of local intelligence—distributed, context-sensitive, and deeply embodied.

That war can stimulate cognitive creativity is an unsettling proposition. We are accustomed to associating creativity with freedom, time, and aesthetic choice. But some of the most consequential innovations in problem-solving have emerged under duress. During World War II, the improvisation of radar jamming technologies, the cryptographic breakthroughs at Bletchley Park, and even the inception of the Manhattan Project all occurred under the shadow of existential urgency. At the individual level, soldiers have recounted solving tactical dilemmas with startling insight—intuition sharpened not by theory but by proximity to death. The difference between breakdown and breakthrough often lies in a single variable: perceived agency. Those who feel powerless tend to collapse. Those who find meaning, even if imposed, are more likely to innovate.

This insight has implications far beyond the battlefield. In contemporary neuroscience and psychology, there is growing interest in the relationship between stress and insight. Some studies suggest that moderate, structured stress—when framed within a sense of purpose—can enhance cognitive flexibility and divergent thinking. This may explain why certain individuals, in wartime and in crisis professions, display elevated performance under pressure. But the line is thin. When stress exceeds the threshold of manageability, it does not sharpen—it shatters. The brain reverts to survival scripts: impulsivity, aggression, withdrawal. Sustained beyond this threshold, it may lead to burnout, dissociation, or psychosis.

The lived accounts of war veterans illustrate this continuum. Some recall moments of near-telepathic clarity, of sensing danger before it appeared, of seeing connections that would never have emerged in civilian life. Others describe complete collapse—cognitive paralysis, emotional flat-lining, or intrusive flashbacks that override present awareness. What makes these accounts powerful is not just their diversity, but their internal contradictions. It is possible for the same mind to oscillate between hyper-functionality and dysfunction within the same hour, sometimes the same minute. This cognitive volatility is a signature of wartime consciousness.

Such volatility can be difficult to integrate post-conflict. The war-trained mind, conditioned to heightened arousal, often finds peacetime intolerably slow, indecisive, or morally ambiguous. Decision-making frameworks built under extreme clarity—where action meant life or death—no longer apply. This mismatch contributes to the sense of alienation many veterans report, not just emotionally, but cognitively. The world no longer makes sense because the brain has been recalibrated for a different kind of sense-making. Reintegration is not merely social—it is neurological.

Understanding this recalibration is essential for developing more effective support systems, not only for veterans, but for any individuals emerging from extreme environments: humanitarian workers, emergency responders, survivors of disasters. The common thread is that their minds have been reshaped by conditions that most people never encounter. They have learned to think in crisis—

sometimes brilliantly, sometimes dysfunctionally, often both. Supporting them requires more than sympathy. It requires *recognition of altered cognition* and the patience to help rebuild trust in slower, less linear forms of thinking.

There is also a philosophical dimension to all this. If the mind is capable of such radical transformation under duress, what does that say about the stability of the self? Are we merely a set of cognitive adaptations tuned to circumstance? Or is there a core—an enduring mental identity—that survives war's distortions? Responses vary. Some argue that trauma reveals the underlying self by stripping away illusion. Others contend that trauma *constructs* the self anew, that identity is formed not before crisis, but through it. Whichever view one takes, the implication is sobering: consciousness is not fixed. Under pressure, it bends.

This chapter does not offer a definitive map of that bending. No such map exists. What it provides is a framework for understanding how crisis acts as both a crucible and a minefield for human cognition. War is not a controlled laboratory. It is an open system—chaotic, reactive, deeply personal. Yet within that system, patterns emerge. Stress rewires the brain. It can sharpen and blunt, build and break. It can destroy memory and produce insight. It can reduce a person to instinct or elevate them to genius. And the same mind can move through all of these states without warning, without logic, and without the luxury of self-explanation.

To study this is not merely to understand war better. It is to understand ourselves—our mental limits, our adaptive capacities, and the fragile interface between thought and environment. In the end, the paradox of cognition under fire is this: the very conditions that threaten to destroy the mind may also be the ones that reveal its most astonishing possibilities.

Empathy in the Enemy's Eyes

In the tightly choreographed theatre of war, empathy is supposed to be a liability—an indulgence that disrupts the binary clarity necessary for combat. Soldiers are trained to dehumanise the enemy, to strip them of personality and motive, to see not a fellow human being but a hostile target. This psychological distancing is not a failure of ethics but a functional necessity for survival and cohesion. And yet, history and field accounts reveal that, under certain conditions, this barrier cracks. In rare and often fleeting moments, combatants report a profound and disarming recognition: a flash of connection with the very person they have been conditioned to kill. These moments do not fit neatly into military narratives or doctrinal analysis. They are ethically untidy, psychologically jarring, and deeply revealing. They tell us something essential—not only about war, but about the stubborn persistence of shared humanity under conditions engineered to suppress it.

Consider the well-documented case of the Christmas Truce in 1914. Along sections of the Western Front, British and German soldiers spontaneously ceased fire, emerging from their trenches to exchange cigarettes, play football, and bury their dead. For a brief time, the social architecture of enmity collapsed. These were not pacifists or ideological dissenters. They were ordinary soldiers, most of them young, many already hardened by the first brutal months of the war. And yet, confronted with the proximity and familiarity of their counterparts—voices in a similar tongue, familiar songs echoing over the wire, the same mud and frost—they experienced not camaraderie, but *recognition*. This was not forgiveness. It was not even agreement. It was something more elemental: the realisation that the enemy was a mirror.

Such incidents, though exceptional, recur throughout military history. During the Second World War, a German sniper was reportedly captured by Allied forces after refusing to shoot a British soldier who reminded him of his brother. In interviews decades later, the sniper—by then a retired postman—struggled to articulate the experience, referring to it only as a "moment when something in me changed shape." In Vietnam, American soldiers spoke of pausing before pulling the trigger upon seeing enemy soldiers doing something banal—smoking, urinating, helping a comrade. The act of seeing the enemy *doing nothing aggressive* seemed to disrupt the internal narrative that permitted lethal action. In these moments, projection collapses. What takes its place is not moral hesitation but emotional dissonance. The frame breaks, and in its place emerges a form of empathy that is not chosen but *imposed* by perception.

From a psychological standpoint, this phenomenon is deeply counterintuitive. Most modern militaries invest considerable effort in depersonalising the adversary. This process, known in military psychology as *deindividuation*, is critical for effective combat. The target becomes an abstraction—a uniform, a silhouette, a dot on a screen. Yet this abstraction requires cognitive effort to maintain, especially in face-to-face combat. When proximity replaces abstraction, the mask slips. The philosopher Emmanuel Levinas famously argued that the human face imposes an ethical demand—the mere presence of another's face calls forth a moral responsibility. Soldiers who report acts of battlefield mercy often cite the moment of visual contact as transformative. The enemy is no longer a concept but a face—and that face destabilises the entire ideological apparatus of war.

It would be tempting to romanticise these encounters as evidence of innate goodness or moral heroism. That would be a mistake. Empathy in war is not always virtuous. It can be confusing, paralysing, even dangerous. Soldiers who spared enemies were sometimes reprimanded or ostracised by their own units. The very act of humanising the enemy can feel like a betrayal—not only of comrades, but of mission. One former Royal Marine described how, after sparing an injured Taliban fighter during a firefight, he was gripped not by relief but by shame. "I saw a kid with fear in his eyes," he recalled, "and I let him crawl away. I still wonder if he came back later and killed one of ours. But at the time, I just couldn't shoot. It wasn't a choice, it just *was*." His commanding officer told him he had failed. The Marine never deployed again. These stories underscore the psychological cost of empathy when it clashes with operational norms and collective identity.

There is also a deeper philosophical question embedded in these moments: what, exactly, is the boundary between self and other? In war, the enemy is defined not by inherent difference but by constructed opposition. The us/them dichotomy is political, strategic, often racialised or nationalistic—but rarely grounded in meaningful difference. Soldiers on opposing sides of a conflict may share more with each other than with the policymakers who sent them to fight. They are often the same age, of similar socioeconomic backgrounds, experiencing the same deprivation, fear, and longing for home. This symmetry becomes intolerable to acknowledge within the logic of war. When it surfaces, it is usually repressed—or remembered only long after the war has ended.

Contemporary neuroscience offers intriguing, if tentative, insights into these encounters. Empathy is not a single capacity but a cluster of neurological processes involving mirror neurons, the prefrontal cortex, and limbic system. Under conditions of stress, the brain often suppresses these circuits to prioritise threat detection. However, intense personalisation—a glimpse of a photograph in a fallen enemy's wallet, a shared gesture, a moment of vulnerability—can reactivate them. The shift is not philosophical but neurological. What begins as a sensory input becomes a moral confrontation. The brain, however primed for aggression, is not immune to recognition.

The implications of this for military training, policy, and rehabilitation are complex. On one hand, militaries cannot function if every soldier is paralysed by the moral ambiguity of their actions. On the other, ignoring or suppressing these humanising moments may contribute to long-term psychological damage. Veterans who engaged in acts of mercy often report these as among the only memories that bring peace. Others who suppressed such impulses sometimes describe lasting feelings of moral dissonance. The presence of empathy, then, is not only a challenge during war—it becomes part of the architecture of recovery after it.

These acts also trouble our moral frameworks. The just war tradition, for example, draws clear lines between combatant and non-combatant, between proportionality and excess. But it does not adequately account for the *unbidden ethical encounters* that arise when those categories blur. What happens when mercy is not strategically justified but *emotionally compelled*? What happens when a soldier acts against orders not out of ideology but because the face before them is too recognisable to destroy?

This ethical tension extends into the domain of drone warfare and remote engagement. As combat becomes increasingly mediated by screens and algorithms, the likelihood of experiencing this kind of empathic rupture diminishes. The soldier operating a drone strike from a base thousands of miles away is insulated from the sensory cues that provoke recognition. There is no face, no gesture, no smell of blood or sound of breathing. As a result, empathy is less likely to emerge. This technological distance may enhance operational efficiency, but it also raises troubling questions about the moral cost of *removing the possibility* of empathic engagement altogether.

And yet, even in these contexts, empathy sometimes finds a way in. There are accounts of drone operators who, after repeated surveillance of targets, developed a psychological attachment—a sense of knowing the patterns and lives of those they watched. Some reported a crisis when eventually ordered to eliminate the very subjects they had come to recognise. The paradox here is acute: technology distances us physically while proximity of observation breeds familiarity. It is a strange inversion, but one that confirms a central point—empathy is not linear. It is situational, relational, often irrational. It cannot be entirely trained out, even in systems designed to suppress it.

To explore these anomalies is not to undermine the necessity of military discipline or the reality of dangerous enemies. It is to understand that beneath uniform and ideology, the basic architecture of human cognition resists perfect dehumanisation. Empathy in war is not a political argument—it is an anthropological and psychological fact. And when it arises, however inconveniently, it challenges the core narrative of total opposition.

Perhaps the most striking feature of these moments is their unpredictability. They cannot be planned or summoned. They occur in the interstices of conflict—when a helmet is removed, when a wound is revealed, when silence momentarily replaces command. These are not moral choices in the abstract. They are eruptions of recognition that demand immediate response. They can save lives. They can cost careers. They can haunt or redeem.

What they always do is reveal the radical contingency of human identity. The enemy is never as fixed as doctrine suggests. Under the right conditions, he becomes a reflection. And in that reflection, some soldiers find not weakness, but clarity—an unsought and fleeting affirmation that, even in the machinery of war, the human mind retains its capacity to see.

The Battlefield as a Laboratory for Self

War memoirs are often shelved under history or military nonfiction, yet many belong more truthfully to the literature of existential inquiry. They are not simply records of combat but of inner dislocation and reckoning. The battlefield becomes, for many who pass through it, a space not only of violence but of radical self-examination. Under the pressure of mortality, stripped of routine and social pretence, individuals confront fundamental questions that in civilian life remain largely deferred: What do I value when everything is at stake? Who am I when fear, loyalty, guilt, and survival contend within a single moment? These are not academic queries. In war, they are lived—brutally, urgently, and often without resolution.

It is for this reason that some of the most philosophically penetrating reflections on meaning, selfhood, and moral clarity have emerged not from universities or think tanks, but from foxholes, POW camps, and after-action reports written in quiet hotel rooms years after the last bullet was fired.

The idea that war strips life down to its existential core is not new. What is less often acknowledged is the extent to which war functions as a *testing ground*—a laboratory in which the self is observed, dismantled, and, in some cases, reforged. The memoirs that emerge from this crucible often reveal more than tactics or trauma; they serve as records of becoming, as documents of how identity is shattered and sometimes reconstructed under the most severe psychological conditions.

Viktor Frankl's *Man's Search for Meaning* stands at the apex of this genre—not because it is the most violent or harrowing, but because it so clearly transforms suffering into inquiry. Although Frankl's imprisonment occurred in Nazi concentration camps, not a formal battlefield, his experience is inseparable from the violence of the Second World War. Frankl, a trained psychiatrist, approached his own suffering with relentless introspection. He noticed that those who survived longest were not always the strongest or healthiest, but those who could *locate meaning* in their suffering—however abstract, future-oriented, or even imaginary that meaning might be. His concept of "tragic optimism"—the belief that life retains potential meaning under even the most miserable conditions—emerged not as a theoretical proposition but as an observational truth. The camp, like the battlefield, became a site where every action, every moment of restraint or collapse, carried existential weight. Frankl's insight was stark: survival is not purely physical. It is interpretative.

Contrast this with Marcus Luttrell's *Lone Survivor*, which recounts a 2005 Navy SEAL mission in Afghanistan that went catastrophically wrong. Luttrell's survival, too, is bound up with meaning, but of a different kind. His account is deeply rooted in codes—of honour, loyalty, sacrifice, and retribution. Where Frankl searched for interior coherence, Luttrell finds identity through the bonds of team and mission. Yet even here, existential questions press in. Why did I live when others died? What am I now that they are gone? How does one return to a civilian life that no longer resembles reality? These are not simply expressions of grief. They are questions about the continuity of the self after extreme experience. Luttrell's narrative is unpolished at times, unapologetically partisan, but it resonates precisely because of its raw moral intensity. Beneath the militarism lies a familiar human struggle: to make sense of survival, to reclaim coherence when the organising structure—war—has disappeared.

War memoirs as existential texts share common features. First, they reject easy narratives of heroism or redemption. Even when acts of courage are described, they are rarely isolated from fear, confusion, or regret. Second, they reveal the instability of identity. Soldiers often report a dissonance between the self they were before deployment, the self they became during war, and the self that attempts to reintegrate afterwards. This fragmentation is not just emotional—it is ontological. Who am I if I have killed? Who am I if I hesitated? Who am I if I survived and others did not? Memoirs often revolve around such questions, not to answer them definitively but to record their enduring presence.

Consider also the lesser-known but equally revealing memoirs such as Edward Tick's *War and the Soul*, or Brian Turner's *My Life as a Foreign Country*, which blend poetry, memory, and philosophical inquiry. Turner, a former US Army infantryman turned poet, writes not only of Iraq but of the psychic continuity between generations of war: his grandfather in WWII, his father in Vietnam, himself in the Middle East. The battlefield becomes both a literal place and a psychological inheritance. His reflections are not about tactics but about the residues of war—the way it enters language, body, and lineage. Turner's work is deeply reflective, often surreal, and committed to the idea that war is not merely experienced but *absorbed*, metabolised slowly over decades, often unconsciously. His writing is evidence of the battlefield as a site of poetic and existential registration.

Even among memoirs more focused on military procedure, moments of existential reflection break through. In *With the Old Breed*, Eugene Sledge recounts his experience in the Pacific theatre during WWII. A disciplined and detailed account of brutality and camaraderie, Sledge's memoir is punctuated by sudden, almost jarring reflections on nature, beauty, and morality. After describing the horrors of Peleliu, he pauses to note the strange serenity of the sky above the carnage, writing, "It seemed incongruous that such a blue sky could preside over so much suffering." These moments are not asides; they are ruptures—points where the machinery of war meets the consciousness of the observer and cannot be reconciled. In that space of dissonance, existential inquiry is born.

The critical function of these memoirs is not simply to tell what happened, but to articulate what *it meant*—and more importantly, what it *did*. They reveal that war does not simply inflict trauma; it generates insight. Not always noble, not always coherent, but insight nonetheless. This insight often emerges through contradiction. A soldier may speak of hating the enemy while also recognising his own brutality. He may speak of brotherhood while recounting acts of betrayal. He may speak of finding purpose while descending into despair. These contradictions are not narrative failures—they are faithful to the complexity of war as lived reality.

In this sense, the battlefield is less a site of transformation than of confrontation. It confronts the individual with aspects of themselves that peacetime may never surface: the capacity for violence, the depths of fear, the nature of loyalty, the elasticity of moral boundaries. Some come to terms with these aspects. Others do not. But either way, the self that emerges is marked—not by ideology, not by nationality, but by *the experience of facing one's limits* and attempting to speak them.

Philosophically, this aligns with existentialist notions of authenticity and freedom. As Jean-Paul Sartre and Simone de Beauvoir argued, true freedom reveals itself under pressure—when one is forced to choose without guarantees. War, with its immediacy and irreversibility, presents such conditions. In the moment before pulling a trigger, in the decision to shield a comrade, or in the silence that follows a morally compromised act, the individual confronts the fact of their own agency. This confrontation is terrifying, but also potentially clarifying. It produces a self-awareness that no training or doctrine can fully prepare for.

Yet the clarity war offers is rarely stable. Most memoirists report not resolution, but an ongoing struggle to integrate their wartime selves into a postwar context that often feels artificial or anaesthetised. Civilian life may appear less vivid, less morally immediate, and in some cases, less *real*. The battlefield's moral stakes, however distorted, were palpable. Decisions mattered immediately. Consequences were lived in the body. This contrast creates a peculiar kind of exile—not from country, but from *normativity*. The memoir, then, becomes a bridge—not only for readers, but for the writers themselves—to revisit, reframe, and possibly reintegrate their fractured selves.

The enduring value of war memoirs lies not only in their witness to history, but in their capacity to pose enduring philosophical questions. They ask what remains of a person after they have been brought to their limit. They expose the fault lines of identity, the elasticity of moral convictions, and the strange alchemy by which purpose and despair often coexist. In doing so, they reveal that the battlefield is not merely a theatre of destruction—it is also, for better or worse, a laboratory for selfhood, where the raw materials of personality are tested by fire and, occasionally, reforged into something new.

Chapter 2
Power, Paranoia, and the Illusion of Control

War has long been told as a story of power—its rise, its application, its ruin. We dress it in the language of military science: force projection, deterrence, command hierarchies. Yet beneath those tidy abstractions lies a more precarious truth. In the theatre of conflict, power is seldom as clean or as steady as it appears in the proclamations of generals or the tidy diagrams of textbooks. It is improvised, emotionally charged, stitched together by perception and belief as much as by material strength. Central to this belief is the comforting fiction that war can be controlled—reduced to rational plans, strategic finesse, or calculated risk. But history is less accommodating. In practice, the machinery of power in war is an unstable alloy of fear, ambition, psychology, and performance. Logic has its place, but so do obsession, insecurity, and the human impulse to read patterns into disorder. The aim here is not to strip power of its usefulness, but to lay bare its fragility.

Strategy, so often celebrated as the spine of military planning, offers a case in point. In theory, it is the realm of clarity and foresight. In practice, it can ossify into something closer to constraint. Napoleon's vaunted manoeuvre warfare—fast, decisive, destabilising—reshaped European conflict. At its inception, it was bold innovation. Yet with time it hardened into orthodoxy, a lens through which he seemed unwilling to adjust his gaze. His Russian campaign exposed the dangers of this strategic rigidity: a brilliant model that faltered against the grind of geography, the stubbornness of culture, and the entropy of logistics. What began as a masterstroke of adaptability calcified into doctrine. In the end, the very belief in his own mastery dulled his ability to see the chaos inherent in the system he commanded.

Modern theorists have tried to account for such realities by borrowing from chaos theory and complexity science. These perspectives accept what military cliché calls the "fog of war" but recast it as an empirical condition: wars are unstable systems, hypersensitive to small variables, prone to wild swings, resistant to centralised control. Reality in the field rarely mirrors the plans drawn up in conference rooms. Soldiers under strain deviate from orders; lines of communication collapse; intelligence proves fragmentary or misleading. The real danger is not that strategy fails to predict every turn—it never could—but that prediction is mistaken for mastery. Every major war contains its moments of improvisation, blind gambles, and instinctive reactions under pressure. The polished image of control comes later, preserved in memoirs, speeches, and national myths.

Few forces warp wartime decision-making more than fear—particularly when it is woven into the structure of policy itself. The Cuban Missile Crisis is remembered as a cool-headed chess match, but the archival record tells a more disquieting tale. Beneath the measured public posture, paranoia seeped into every crevice. Decisions were shaped not only by the desire to avoid war but by the need to project strength, maintain political standing, satisfy hawkish advisers, and shield the leader's own image. Surveillance photographs were misread; messages went astray; intent was guessed at rather than known. That the world skirted so close to nuclear disaster owed less to the precision of strategic alignment than to the unpredictable behaviour of complex systems under stress. Paranoia, in that moment, was not an outlier—it was baked into the Cold War machine.

This is the uncomfortable truth: fear is not a blemish on leadership—it is often its fuel. When it becomes normalised, it bends policy itself. Traditional political science, with its rational actor models, struggles to account for this. Such models assume coherence, careful cost–benefit weighing, a steady hand on the tiller. Yet history is strewn with decisions that defy those assumptions. Leaders prolong losing wars not because victory is plausible but because retreat would be a psychic humiliation. Campaigns are sustained for reasons of legacy, ego, or ideological purity. These are not lapses in reason—they are the workings of a different logic, one rooted in the subconscious, the symbolic, and the performative.

To grasp power in war is to recognise its theatrical dimension. Leadership in these moments is as much stagecraft as it is execution.

Reputation, precedent, and the projection of resolve shape actions as surely as battlefield reports. Churchill grasped this instinctively. His wartime broadcasts were not dry briefings; they were scaffolding for the national spirit. His voice carried a persona designed not just for domestic resolve but for foreign eyes—to suggest that surrender was beyond contemplation. This was leadership as emotional engineering, steeped in symbolism and finely tuned rhetoric.

Lincoln, during the American Civil War, wielded political theatre with equal deliberation. The Emancipation Proclamation was at once a moral act and a calculated manoeuvre: it reframed the war's purpose, undercut potential European support for the Confederacy, and boosted Union morale. To acknowledge its strategic purpose is not to strip it of moral weight, but to recognise how morality itself can be marshalled as an instrument of war. The most effective wartime leaders are rarely the most clinically rational—they are those attuned to narrative, emotion, and the shifting moods within and beyond their own command.

This unsettles the neat frameworks that still underpin much international relations theory. The rational actor model, though repeatedly critiqued, continues to haunt analysis. It assumes states behave like calculating individuals—sizing up risks, seeking optimal outcomes. But the record says otherwise. The 2003 invasion of Iraq was propelled by a tangle of ideology, misjudgement, bureaucratic drift, and the unconscious pull of confirming pre-existing beliefs. Intelligence was not merely manipulated but shaped by what decision-makers wanted to believe. Groupthink, rivalries, and performative certainty all played their part. The cloak of rationality remained; the machinery beneath it was volatile and often irrational.

Decisions in war are forged under the least ideal conditions imaginable—compressed timelines, fractured intelligence, political distortion, and the dread of reputational collapse. The individuals making them are not abstract "actors" but people: susceptible to bias, driven by pride, swayed by emotion, navigating murky ethics. Power here is not simply about issuing commands; it is about managing uncertainty while projecting confidence. Sometimes it even means cultivating unpredictability—projecting instability as a deterrent. In this sense, the logic of power can include the deliberate performance of madness.

This chapter will explore four interlocking dimensions of that reality. First, how strategy—originally a tool of clarity—can congeal into a form of blindness. Second, how paranoia functions not as a flaw but as a governing principle. Third, how leadership in war operates as a sequence of performances, where emotion and symbolism are wielded as weapons. Finally, how the myth of the rational actor crumbles when tested against the heat and ambiguity of real wartime decision-making. These threads are not relics of the past; they remain stitched into today's architecture of global security, where deterrence, perception, and the management of unpredictability still govern the most dangerous levers of statecraft.

Seeing war in this light does nothing to make it less alarming. On the contrary, it strips away the reassuring belief that leaders always know what they are doing, that systems respond predictably, or that reason inevitably holds sway in the gravest of decisions. Yet it does offer a clearer vantage—one grounded in psychological realism, historical record, and moral nuance. From there, perhaps, emerges a more candid form of security policy and leadership. Not flawless, certainly. But less enamoured of their own myths, and—just possibly—wiser within the limits of control.

The Tyranny of Strategy

Strategy, by definition, is meant to clarify. It promises to bring coherence to complexity, direction to uncertainty, and mastery over chaos. In theory, it disciplines instinct, tempers impulsiveness, and offers a structured path to victory. Yet in practice, strategy often does something else: it creates blind spots, calcifies assumptions, and seduces decision-makers into believing that war is more knowable and controllable than it actually is. When strategy hardens into orthodoxy—when it is wielded as a template rather than a tool—it becomes a liability. This is the paradox at the heart of military planning: the very frameworks designed to anticipate complexity can become mechanisms for ignoring it. Nowhere is this more apparent than in the study of overreliance on strategic models that privilege pattern over unpredictability, coherence over contingency, and doctrine over discretion.

Napoleon Bonaparte remains one of the most celebrated strategists in military history. His mastery of manoeuvre warfare—the use of rapid, flexible, and decentralised movement to overwhelm the enemy—transformed European battlefields. His early campaigns, particularly in Italy and Austerlitz, demonstrated extraordinary innovation. He exploited terrain, timing, and psychological pressure with surgical precision. But as his ambitions expanded, so too did his attachment to a specific way of winning. Manoeuvre became not a means, but a mindset—an ideological commitment that eventually rendered him blind to its limits. During the ill-fated Russian campaign of 1812, Napoleon attempted to apply his familiar model to a theatre that defied it. Vast distances, logistical fragility, and a noncompliant enemy dissolved his assumptions. He pursued mobility into an environment where mobility was meaningless. What had once been brilliance became repetition. His strategy, elegant in theory, could not metabolise the chaos it encountered. His failure was not tactical. It was conceptual.

This pattern has recurred throughout modern warfare. Strategic doctrines—whether based on mobility, deterrence, attrition, or counterinsurgency—often emerge from previous successes and quickly ossify into dogma. In the First World War, the cult of the offensive—rooted in 19th-century ideas about morale and elan—led to catastrophic losses as generals persisted with frontal assaults against entrenched positions. The Maginot Line, France's post-WWI defensive strategy, exemplified the dangers of fighting the last war. Designed to prevent a repeat of German invasion through fixed fortifications, it was easily bypassed by German tanks using a strategy of *blitzkrieg*—a model predicated precisely on the kind of operational speed and fluidity that the Maginot Line could not address. Strategic foresight, in these cases, gave way to strategic inertia.

One of the underlying reasons for this strategic rigidity is the cognitive appeal of frameworks. Humans—and institutions—are psychologically inclined to prefer structure over flux. Strategic models offer not just planning tools, but psychological reassurance. They reduce anxiety by transforming war, which is inherently unpredictable, into something that feels procedural. Military training reflects this: simulations, checklists, decision trees. The abstraction of strategy becomes a comfort against the messiness of actual battle. Yet this abstraction often fails to translate into the battlefield's erratic tempo, its nonlinear feedback loops, or the unpredictability of human behaviour under pressure.

Chaos theory, while not a traditional military discipline, provides a useful lens through which to understand the limits of rigid strategy. Originally developed in mathematics and physics, chaos theory explores how systems that are deterministic in their rules can nonetheless behave unpredictably due to extreme sensitivity to initial conditions. The classic metaphor—the flap of a butterfly's wings triggering a distant hurricane—has clear analogues in war. A misheard order, a sudden weather shift, a junior officer's improvisation, or the death of a single operative can cascade into dramatically altered outcomes. Clausewitz alluded to this in his notion of "friction"—the inevitable gap between plan and execution. Chaos theory offers a more granular and mathematically grounded way of understanding that gap. It tells us that small deviations, once they begin, do not simply create inconvenience. They can dismantle the entire operational architecture.

In this sense, the battlefield is not a chessboard, as classical strategy would suggest. It is a complex adaptive system. Units interact in unpredictable ways. Information is partial. Decision-making is distributed. Feedback loops abound. Linear models—A leads to B leads to C—fail to capture this. What results is not disorder in the colloquial sense, but *nonlinearity*: situations where outcomes are not proportional to inputs, where minor actors can exert major influence, and where plans fail not because they were flawed in detail, but because they relied on an imagined stability that never existed.

The American involvement in Vietnam offers a modern case study in this disjunction. The U.S. military, guided by metrics-based strategy—body counts, kill ratios, territorial control—approached the conflict with a strategic framework designed for conventional warfare. But the insurgency, sustained by local networks, asymmetrical tactics, and political legitimacy in rural areas, rendered these metrics irrelevant. Strategic clarity gave way to strategic delusion. By measuring success through quantifiable outputs, military planners missed the qualitative shifts occurring on the ground. Strategy persisted, but reality diverged. The illusion of control—fuelled by data, models, and doctrine—obscured the adaptive capacity of the opponent.

To be clear, the problem is not strategy itself. Strategy is indispensable. But its tyranny emerges when it becomes prescriptive rather than responsive, when it closes off feedback rather than inviting it. Good strategy acknowledges its own limits. It creates space for revision, for bottom-up innovation, for the unexpected. It builds adaptability into its core assumptions. And yet, in most wartime bureaucracies, the opposite occurs. Strategy is treated as a contract with reality. Deviation is punished. Flexibility is mistaken for weakness. Hierarchies demand certainty, and certainty breeds overconfidence.

This is where leadership intersects with strategy. The most effective wartime leaders—Napoleon at his best, Lincoln during the Civil War, even Eisenhower on D-Day—did not merely follow strategic doctrine. They read the pattern and then broke it. They treated strategy as a conversation, not a decree. They understood that control was partial, that the battlefield would distort whatever they imagined, and that their job was to listen as much as direct. Their genius lay not in doctrinal purity but in situational fluency.

The post-9/11 wars further expose the tyranny of strategic orthodoxy. In Afghanistan and Iraq, successive strategies—clear, hold, build; troop surges; decapitation strikes—were developed with logical consistency but often failed to anticipate how local actors would adapt. Taliban fighters melted into civilian populations. Insurgent groups fractured and reassembled. Strategic success in one province led to new insurgencies elsewhere. The system absorbed and redirected pressure in ways that linear models could not anticipate. Strategy, in these theatres, often meant chasing stability in a system designed to resist it.

What this suggests is that strategy must be reconceived not as a blueprint but as an evolving hypothesis. It must be falsifiable, responsive to anomalies, and embedded within a culture of critical feedback. This is not how strategy is typically taught. The allure of grand theories—Sun Tzu, Clausewitz, Jomini—remains powerful. But the battlefield no longer grants the luxury of static doctrine. Digital communication, hybrid warfare, disinformation campaigns, and decentralised threats demand a different mindset: one that treats unpredictability as a feature, not a flaw.

There is also an ethical dimension to this. The tyranny of strategy can become the tyranny of abstraction—where civilian casualties are justified by "operational necessity," where long-term consequences are discounted because they fall outside the model's time horizon, where local knowledge is ignored because it disrupts the narrative coherence of the plan. Strategy, when unmoored from its human consequences, becomes a form of moral insulation. It allows decision-makers to distance themselves from the realities their decisions produce. This is not a flaw of individual character. It is a structural effect of thinking through frameworks that prize optimisation over experience.

To liberate strategy from its own tyranny is not to discard it. It is to humanise it. To recognise that no model survives contact with the full complexity of war, and that wisdom lies not in tighter control, but in deeper attentiveness. Chaos theory reminds us that systems behave in strange and sometimes beautiful ways. Strategy must learn to do the same. It must embrace uncertainty not as a threat to authority, but as a source of insight. Only then can it serve its original purpose: not to impose order, but to make sense of disorder without becoming captive to it.

When Fear Becomes Policy

Paranoia in foreign policy is often dismissed as a failure of leadership or a quirk of ideology, a distortion of otherwise rational statecraft. Yet closer scrutiny reveals something far more unsettling: paranoia is not a deviation from strategic logic—it is often its foundation. In the modern security state, fear is institutionalised, systematised, and treated not as an aberration, but as a prerequisite for vigilance. The Cold War crystallised this dynamic, but it did not invent it. What it did was expose, in full view, the structural incentives for worst-case thinking, anticipatory aggression, and the choreography of mistrust. The Cuban Missile Crisis is frequently remembered as a case study in crisis management and nuclear restraint. But beneath the mythology lies a deeper truth: the event revealed how policy at the highest levels of global power was shaped less by information than by imagination—by the perceived intentions of the enemy, by unverified assumptions, and by the psychological gravitational pull of fear. It was not a test of pure rationality; it was a dance of mutual paranoia—calculated, rehearsed, and only barely restrained.

By the autumn of 1962, the United States and the Soviet Union had constructed foreign policy architectures that depended on the assumption of adversarial intent. Strategic doctrines like "massive retaliation," "flexible response," and "mutually assured destruction" (MAD) were not simply reactive positions—they were predicated on the belief that the enemy was always seeking an advantage, even if no evidence of such advantage was available. Fear was not an intermittent emotional state; it was a constant operational framework. Intelligence reports, military exercises, and diplomatic briefings were all interpreted through a lens of anticipatory suspicion. The discovery of Soviet missile installations in Cuba did not trigger a response merely because of their offensive potential, but because they confirmed an already entrenched belief that the Soviets were methodically tightening a noose around the American homeland. The strategic significance of the missiles was debatable—the United States already faced nuclear threats from Soviet submarines and ICBMs—but the psychological significance was absolute. They represented proximity, surprise, and humiliation. And for policymakers conditioned by Cold War logic, *those* were the real threats.

What followed was not an exercise in calm rationality, but a high-stakes theatre of control, in which miscommunication, false signals, and emotional pressure nearly led to nuclear war. President Kennedy's Executive Committee of the National Security Council (ExComm) was divided between hawks, who favoured immediate military strikes, and moderates advocating a naval blockade. What's notable is that both sides operated on worst-case assumptions. The hawks believed in Soviet duplicity and viewed negotiation as a trap. The moderates feared escalation, but did not discount the possibility that the Soviets might be irrational enough to launch. At several points, decisions were based not on evidence, but on *what the other side might believe about us*. This recursive logic—second-guessing an adversary's second-guessing—created a feedback loop in which certainty became elusive, and action increasingly dictated by fear of appearing weak.

One of the most chilling moments came when a Soviet submarine commander, out of radio contact and believing war had already begun, prepared to launch a nuclear torpedo. The action was only averted because of the dissent of a single officer, Vasili Arkhipov, who refused to confirm the launch order. This near-catastrophic misunderstanding did not occur because either side intended to escalate, but because the systems in place *assumed* escalation was always imminent. The crisis ended through a negotiated withdrawal of Soviet missiles from Cuba and, covertly, American missiles from Turkey. But the mythology of Kennedy's steely resolve and Khrushchev's rational backdown obscures the more complex truth: both leaders were reacting to internal dynamics of institutionalised fear. Their publics, their advisers, and their militaries all operated within ecosystems that rewarded suspicion and punished perceived softness.

This is not a critique of Cold War leadership per se. It is a critique of the *systemic logic* that made fear the dominant currency of policy. The political scientist Robert Jervis referred to this as the "security dilemma"—a situation in which measures taken by one state to increase its own security are interpreted as threats by others, leading to escalation. But this dilemma is not just a theoretical construct. It has been built into the architecture of state behaviour through bureaucratic incentives, intelligence biases, and the imperative of credibility. To show doubt, to question assumptions, or to propose empathy with an adversary is often seen as naivety or betrayal. In such environments, paranoia is not irrational—it is *rationalised.* It is baked into models, war games, and strategic forecasts.

The result is a policymaking culture that begins not with possibility, but with threat. During the early years of the Reagan administration, intelligence estimates consistently exaggerated Soviet military spending and aggressiveness. These projections shaped defence budgets, diplomatic posture, and domestic political rhetoric. Only years later did declassified documents reveal the extent to which Soviet leaders, particularly under Brezhnev, were operating from a position of defensive insecurity rather than expansionist ambition. But once institutional narratives are formed, they are difficult to dislodge. Threat inflation becomes self-reinforcing. Budgets, reputations, and political capital become tied to particular readings of the enemy's intent.

Modern counterterrorism policies exhibit similar tendencies. The architecture of the post-9/11 security state—surveillance programmes, targeted killings, indefinite detention—was justified through a logic of *pre-emption.* The enemy might be anywhere, planning anything. And because the risk of inaction was framed as existential, the threshold for evidence was lowered. Guantánamo Bay became not just a prison, but a symbol of a policy approach that equated uncertainty with imminent threat. Once again, paranoia was operationalised—not as failure, but as prudence.

This is not to say that fear has no place in policy. Threats are real. States must be vigilant. But when fear becomes the dominant epistemology—when it determines not only how we act, but how we *interpret*—it corrodes the capacity for strategic flexibility. It creates environments in which dialogue is interpreted as deception, ambiguity as aggression, and restraint as weakness. The escalation risks of this mindset are not hypothetical. The 1983 NATO exercise "Able Archer" simulated a nuclear conflict in a way that Soviet intelligence interpreted as a possible first strike. For several days, Soviet forces were on alert, and once again, nuclear war became a distinct possibility—not because of intention, but because of imagination.

The psychological drivers of this logic are well documented. Prospect theory, developed by Daniel Kahneman and Amos Tversky, demonstrates that decision-makers tend to overweigh potential losses relative to gains. In security policy, this means that the fear of losing strategic advantage often outweighs the desire to build cooperative frameworks. Additionally, groupthink dynamics within elite circles can amplify these tendencies. Leaders are surrounded by advisers incentivised to confirm assumptions, to overstate risks, and to privilege loyalty over dissent. In such conditions, rationality does not vanish. It simply *recalibrates* around threat.

One of the more disturbing implications of this is that peace itself can be destabilising. When adversaries show signs of moderation or reform, these gestures may be viewed with suspicion. Nixon's opening to China, though ultimately transformative, was initially resisted by many within his own administration as dangerously trusting. The 2015 Iran nuclear deal was met with fierce opposition, not necessarily because of its terms, but because it disrupted the prevailing narrative of the Iranian regime as permanently irrational and implacably hostile. Paranoia resists de-escalation because de-escalation undermines the psychological and bureaucratic foundations upon which decades of threat perception have been built.

To understand when fear becomes policy is to understand the political utility of paranoia. It provides justification for extraordinary measures, budgets, surveillance, and intervention. It allows leaders to consolidate authority by externalising threats. It transforms uncertainty into mandate. But this comes at a cost—not just in resources, but in imagination. When policy is shaped primarily by the anticipation of worst-case scenarios, the range of possible futures narrows. Innovation becomes dangerous. Dialogue becomes appeasement. Complexity becomes threat.

The challenge, then, is not to eliminate fear from policymaking. That would be naive. The challenge is to *discipline* it—to recognise when vigilance slips into obsession, when caution morphs into hostility, and when the feedback loops of mistrust become self-fulfilling. Historical hindsight is often harsh on leaders who hesitated. But rarely does it account for the courage required to resist the momentum of institutionalised paranoia. The most dangerous policies are often not driven by hatred, ideology, or aggression—but by fear masquerading as logic. Understanding this is not just an academic exercise. It is a prerequisite for more honest, and ultimately more effective, security thinking.

Leadership in the Abyss

Leadership under the conditions of war is not a test of procedural competence. It is a confrontation with chaos. In this space, traditional assumptions about rationality and decision-making collapse under pressure, and the leaders who succeed are rarely those who follow orthodox models of command. They are those who recognise that logic alone is insufficient to bind fractured societies, navigate internal dissent, or interpret ambiguous signals from the enemy. Instead, wartime leadership frequently demands counterintuitive moves—emotional performance, symbolic acts, selective deception, theatrical gestures, and the deliberate bending of established norms to reframe meaning. To lead in war is not only to decide, but to *shape perception.* This is not weakness. It is strategy. And understanding it requires moving beyond technocratic definitions of leadership into the murkier terrain where emotion, myth, and moral uncertainty are core instruments of statecraft.

Winston Churchill is often caricatured as the quintessential wartime bulldog: defiant, witty, strategically astute. Yet his most enduring legacy lies not in battlefield brilliance, but in the emotional architecture he constructed through language and image. In 1940, Britain stood largely alone against Hitler's Wehrmacht. The rational response might have been negotiation. Britain had suffered significant losses in France, and a German invasion seemed plausible, even imminent. Yet Churchill, newly installed as Prime Minister, rejected not only appeasement but the *frame* in which appeasement made sense. His speeches were less about policy and more about reshaping collective psychology. Phrases like "their finest hour" or "we shall fight on the beaches" were not tactical directives—they were myth-making devices. He used cadence, metaphor, and defiance to generate a moral narrative in which continued resistance felt not just necessary but inevitable. This was emotional manipulation by design. Churchill understood that morale was not merely a byproduct of confidence, but something that could be engineered. In doing so, he redefined the role of the wartime leader—not just as strategist-in-chief, but as a kind of national dramaturge, orchestrating sentiment as much as policy.

A century earlier, Abraham Lincoln confronted a different abyss: civil war, institutional fracture, and moral ambiguity over the future of the American republic. His leadership, particularly during the early 1860s, defies easy classification. He was neither doctrinaire nor predictable. He suspended habeas corpus, delayed emancipation until it could serve both moral and military objectives, and constantly recalibrated his positions in response to the pressures of battlefield developments and political necessity. Critics then and now have debated whether Lincoln was guided more by principle or expediency. What emerges upon close study is not duplicity, but *strategic theatricality*. Lincoln's use of public letters, satirical parables, and carefully staged cabinet debates created an aura of transparency even as he manoeuvred behind the scenes. The Gettysburg Address, with its sparse elegance, condensed centuries of philosophical argument into under 300 words—not as a description of the present, but as a retroactive consecration of meaning onto a chaotic war. Lincoln used language not to report reality but to reshape it, binding disparate factions under a vision of purpose that only emerged *after* the fact.

Both Churchill and Lincoln grasped something often ignored in conventional leadership theory: that belief must be cultivated, not merely inherited. When people are afraid, fragmented, and fatigued, they do not respond to cold calculus. They respond to coherence—narratives that make sense of suffering, losses that appear redemptive, and actions that feel symbolically resonant. This is not to suggest that rationality disappears, but that it is necessarily supplemented—by affect, performance, and the intuitive reading of collective mood. The best wartime leaders are not only decision-makers; they are narrators of meaning.

This contradicts the dominant model in political science: the rational actor framework, which assumes that leaders act to maximise utility within a stable set of preferences. In war, these assumptions collapse. Preferences are fluid. Information is incomplete. And outcomes are judged retrospectively, often with distorted hindsight. Take Franklin

D. Roosevelt's leadership during World War II. His decision to prioritise the European theatre before engaging the Pacific fully, to offer lend-lease aid before entering the war formally, and to pursue an alliance with Stalin despite deep ideological divisions—none of these moves were straightforward. Internally, Roosevelt operated through ambiguity. He preserved multiple options, manipulated timelines, and often allowed subordinates to believe they had shaped policy that he had already decided. His success lay in the ability to delay closure, to stretch ambiguity until the political conditions allowed action. This was not indecision. It was *management of temporal perception*. Roosevelt understood that in wartime, timing was not merely tactical—it was existential.

Modern examples reinforce the complexity of wartime leadership. Consider Volodymyr Zelenskyy's decision, in the first days of Russia's full-scale invasion of Ukraine in 2022, to remain in Kyiv when evacuation was offered. The decision had no immediate military value. Zelenskyy was not a general. His death or capture would have had catastrophic consequences. Rational risk assessment would have favoured retreat. But the symbolic impact of remaining—of filming his nighttime messages in the streets, of declaring "I need ammunition, not a ride"—reoriented Ukraine's narrative overnight. It signalled defiance, unity, and a refusal to cede moral ground. This was leadership through performance, through the careful use of presence as politics. It demonstrates that the battlefield includes not just terrain and weaponry, but imagination, visibility, and posture.

Critics often deride this kind of leadership as theatrical, implying superficiality. But such critiques misunderstand the stakes. Theatre in war is not decoration. It is a mechanism for anchoring behaviour. When morale is fragile and loyalties frayed, *symbols do more than speeches*. They encode commitment, mobilise identity, and create emotional scaffolding for policy. Napoleon's eagle standards, Roosevelt's fireside chats, de Gaulle's broadcasts from London—all of these were theatrical in form, but strategic in effect. They transmitted confidence, summoned collective will, and rendered abstract objectives emotionally graspable.

This raises a deeper challenge to leadership orthodoxy: what if decisiveness is less important than interpretive capacity? Traditional metrics of leadership—speed of decision, clarity of objective, command of detail—are necessary but insufficient. What matters equally is the capacity to read uncertainty, to tolerate ambiguity, to adjust frames. This interpretive skill is rarely taught in military academies or business schools, but it is vital in contexts where no move is obviously right, where information is contradictory, and where time pressure distorts judgment. In these moments, leaders are not merely problem-solvers—they are *meaning-makers*, operating in a semiotic field of gesture, signal, expectation, and doubt.

Yet leadership in the abyss is not without cost. The same qualities that produce wartime effectiveness—emotional command, symbolic deftness, theatrical presence—can become liabilities in peacetime. Churchill was unceremoniously voted out of office in 1945. Lincoln was assassinated before Reconstruction revealed the limitations of his moral narrative. Leaders shaped by existential conflict often find themselves maladapted to normalcy. Their talents are forged in rupture, not routine. This makes them both essential and expendable—heroes in crisis, but ambiguous figures in stability.

What can we extract from this for broader understanding? First, that wartime leadership cannot be fully captured by procedural or managerial models. It is psychological, symbolic, and often paradoxical. Second, that rationality, while important, is mediated by emotion, timing, and cultural narrative. The leaders who endure are not always the most consistent or the most principled, but those who *understand what is required in the moment*—and who can make that requirement appear historically inevitable. Third, that leadership in war demands both a grasp of logistics and a feel for myth. Without the former, nothing functions. Without the latter, nothing holds.

To lead in the abyss is to construct meaning when facts are incomplete, to persuade when the path is unclear, and to act not despite uncertainty, but *because* of it. It is a discipline of paradox. And for that reason, it remains one of the most complex and consequential human capacities. Understanding how such leadership works—beyond caricature, beyond cliché—is essential not only to grasp the history of war, but to prepare for the future crises where leadership may again be all that stands between collapse and coherence.

The Myth of the Rational Actor

The rational actor model has served as the intellectual scaffolding for much of modern political science and strategic theory. It assumes that state behaviour, especially in matters of war and peace, can be modelled as a sequence of calculated decisions made by coherent actors maximising their interests under conditions of uncertainty. This framework underpins Cold War nuclear strategy, decision theory, game theory, and vast swathes of international relations literature. It offers clarity, elegance, and a comforting sense of order—where motivations are legible, preferences stable, and choices traceable to identifiable goals. But in the real world of wartime decision-making, this model is not just inaccurate; it is dangerously misleading. Decisions in war are rarely made under ideal conditions. They are shaped by emotion, ego, misperception, internal group dynamics, and unconscious drives. The rational actor is not merely a simplification—it is a fiction. And continuing to treat it as a reliable guide to state behaviour in conflict obscures the deeper psychological and institutional forces at play.

Consider the United States' decision to enter the Vietnam War. Classical readings, grounded in rationalist models, often describe this as an attempt to contain communism, preserve regional alliances, and uphold credibility in line with the domino theory. But a closer examination of internal communications—memos, transcripts, and testimonies—reveals a more troubling picture. Many within the

Johnson administration doubted the war's winnability from the outset. Decision-making was not driven by clear goals or cost-benefit logic, but by fear of appearing weak, by reputational anxiety, and by bureaucratic inertia. Once a particular narrative—Vietnam as a linchpin of global containment—had taken root, dislodging it became politically impossible. Rationality did not govern the decision to escalate. *Fear of the domestic consequences of withdrawal* did. As Daniel Ellsberg, one of the architects of early Vietnam policy, later admitted, "We always knew the war was unwinnable, but no one wanted to be the one who lost it."

This form of irrationality is not random. It is *structured*—rooted in predictable psychological patterns that affect individuals and institutions alike. Cognitive biases such as loss aversion, confirmation bias, and the sunk cost fallacy are now well documented in behavioural economics. Yet their implications for wartime decision-making remain insufficiently explored. Leaders frequently cling to flawed policies not because they believe in their success, but because abandoning them would mean acknowledging failure. The rational actor model has no room for this kind of pride, shame, or symbolic accountability. But history is replete with leaders who escalate not because the odds are favourable, but because retreat threatens their identity, legacy, or domestic authority.

One of the most widely studied cases of supposedly rational crisis management—the Cuban Missile Crisis—also reveals the limitations of the model when examined in detail. Official narratives often present President Kennedy as a cool-headed strategist who balanced military pressure with diplomatic restraint to avert nuclear war. But newly released tapes of ExComm meetings reveal an atmosphere of confusion, emotion, and internal conflict. Options were debated not in linear fashion, but through overlapping fears, political calculations, and personality clashes. Several proposed actions, including an immediate airstrike on Cuba, were based on worst-case assumptions rather than verified intelligence. Kennedy's eventual decision to impose a naval blockade and secretly agree to remove

U.S. missiles from Turkey was not the product of game-theoretic rationality, but of a layered compromise—a mix of political optics, personal instinct, and backchannel improvisation. The outcome was successful, but the process was anything but clean.

The foundational error of the rational actor model is that it mistakes coherence for reality. It imposes clarity onto a domain defined by ambiguity. In real wartime contexts, actors are not unitary. States are coalitions of agencies, interest groups, ideologues, and egos. Decisions emerge not from a central calculating brain but from fragmented institutions engaged in competition, performance, and negotiation. Graham Allison's "bureaucratic politics" model, developed in the aftermath of the Cuban Missile Crisis, made this point decades ago. Yet the field continues to revert to rational actor assumptions, in part because they are easier to model, teach, and simulate. Complexity resists simplification—but simplification is what policymakers crave when under pressure.

Rationality also assumes information symmetry and internal consistency. In practice, wartime decisions are made with partial data, distorted by ideology, filtered through multiple layers of analysis, and interpreted according to the political needs of the moment. The 2003 invasion of Iraq was justified largely on the premise of weapons of mass destruction, despite significant dissent within the intelligence community. That dissent was suppressed, not because it lacked substance, but because it contradicted the preferred narrative. Rational actor logic would predict that if key evidence is weak or falsifiable, the policy would adjust. In reality, evidence was *reshaped to fit the policy*. Intelligence became advocacy. Strategic communication replaced deliberation. Decisions were made first and justified later. Here again, rationality was not absent—it was *performed* after the fact to maintain legitimacy.

It is also worth considering the role of unconscious psychological forces—narcissism, projection, trauma, and identification—in the making of war. Psychoanalytic readings of leaders such as Adolf

Hitler, Joseph Stalin, or even Richard Nixon offer unsettling insights. These men were not irrational in the sense of being chaotic or incompetent. But their strategic decisions were filtered through personal pathologies—grandiosity, paranoia, obsession—that shaped their worldview and drove them to seek symbolic victories over adversaries imagined as existential threats. The rational actor model cannot accommodate such forces. It assumes transparency of motive. But leadership in war often involves *concealed motives*—not only from the public but from the leader themselves. When George W. Bush described his decision to invade Iraq as "gut-level," he was not speaking metaphorically. He was articulating something real: that leadership decisions are often affective before they are analytical.

Even collective decision-making bodies are not immune. Cabinet dynamics, national security councils, and military leadership teams all exhibit groupthink, hierarchy-induced silence, and status preservation. The Falklands War, initiated in part because Margaret Thatcher's cabinet perceived the need to demonstrate British resolve in the post-imperial era, was not a purely rational strategic choice. It was a conflict shaped by symbolic politics, domestic pressure, and the need to reaffirm national identity. The success of the war bolstered Thatcher's leadership, but the decision to enter it was fraught with uncertainty and contradictory advice. As with so many wars, its rationale crystallised only after the fact.

This retrospective imposition of coherence is a final indictment of the rational actor model. It encourages a kind of historical revisionism in which events appear inevitable, and decisions appear well-founded. But such coherence is an illusion crafted through narrative. Actual wartime decision-making is fluid, contingent, and often improvisational. Leaders do not possess perfect information, stable preferences, or unlimited time. They rely on instinct, experience, advisors, emotion, and the political constraints of the moment. What appears rational in hindsight was frequently a gamble in real time.

Rejecting the myth of the rational actor is not a call for cynicism. It is an invitation to build models that reflect human reality. This means incorporating insights from psychology, organisational theory, and history. It means recognising that strategic choices are embedded in emotional contexts. It means treating states not as unified calculators but as arenas of conflict and contestation. And it means accepting that war is not the domain of pure logic, but of deeply human impulses—some noble, some delusional, all consequential.

To understand war, we must understand how decisions are really made—not how we wish they were made, not how textbooks describe them, but how they unfold in the heat of ambiguity, fear, pride, and hope. The rational actor model has served its time. What we need now is a theory of decision-making robust enough to contain contradiction, chaos, and the full range of human behaviour under stress. Only then can our understanding of war move from abstraction to accuracy—and perhaps, from repetition to restraint.

Chapter 3
Innovation Under Fire: How Catastrophe Breeds Creativity

The old adage that war is the mother of invention is often repeated with a kind of fatalistic shrug, yet it is rarely unpacked. Embedded in it is a stark recognition: humanity's most significant leaps—whether technological, organisational, or philosophical—are often coaxed not from stability, but from collapse. Calamity doesn't simply speed along existing trajectories; it alters the very soil in which ideas take root. In peace, innovation tends to be domesticated—harnessed to budgets, committees, feasibility studies, and regulatory review. In war, when failure is not a matter of lost investment but of lives cut short, those tethers are slashed. Entire ways of thinking are suspended, replaced by an improvisational urgency where the improbable is demanded and the impossible is, somehow, brought into being. The real question is not only what emerges from such periods, but why destruction so reliably breeds creation.

Consider the Second World War. Radar, antibiotics, the jet engine—all reached operational maturity in shockingly short order. These were not lucky accidents; they were the product of focused, unrelenting scientific labour in conditions where failure was inconceivable. Radar, for instance, had been an intriguing possibility before the conflict, but in Britain it became an imperative. With the Luftwaffe conducting nightly raids, the Telecommunications Research Establishment's scientists could ill afford leisurely inquiry. Physicists, engineers, and military planners set aside their disciplinary fences and worked shoulder-to-shoulder. The result was more than a technological breakthrough; it was a case study in boundary-crossing collaboration, the sort of trespass only desperation could sanction.

Penicillin tells a parallel story. Alexander Fleming had discovered it in 1928, but for over a decade it remained little more than a laboratory curiosity. The Second World War altered that calculus entirely. With battlefield infections ravaging soldiers, patience became a luxury no one could afford. Under the stewardship of

Howard Florey and Ernst Chain, production was scaled at unprecedented speed. What had been an underutilised marvel was transformed into a mass-produced medical staple precisely because war redefined delay as a kind of defeat. Wartime urgency did not simply accelerate the drug's arrival—it rewrote the pace of medical progress itself.

Innovation, however, often unfolds beyond the laboratory bench. Wars also reshape the hidden architectures of supply, transport, and communication. The U.S. Interstate Highway System owes much to the logistical lessons of World War II, when moving men and machines revealed the fragility of existing roads. That experience directly informed Eisenhower's post-war infrastructure push. Similarly, the internet's precursor, ARPANET, was born of Cold War fears—a decentralised network designed to survive nuclear attack. Civilian uses came later, but they were built atop a foundation designed to endure catastrophe. In both cases, infrastructure was imagined through the lens of vulnerability, not convenience.

The freedom war grants innovators is a double-edged gift. It can mean liberation from bureaucracy, but also from moral restraint. The Manhattan Project, bringing together minds like Oppenheimer, Fermi, Szilard, and Bohr, would likely have been slowed to a crawl in peacetime. In war, it became coherent—and lethal. The bomb's creation was both a scientific triumph and an ethical abyss. This is the uneasy truth: invention born in crisis is morally agnostic, capable of delivering emancipation or annihilation with equal ease.

Some of the most radical wartime breakthroughs occur not in machines, but in minds. At Bletchley Park, Britain's codebreaking hub, Alan Turing and his peers worked not only to crack the Enigma cipher but to reimagine the very nature of thought. Turing's notion that machines could simulate human reasoning was not a philosophical whim—it was a weapon. In an environment where encrypted messages could determine the fate of thousands, abstract computation became a matter of life and death. Today's AI debates still bear the imprint of that moment, when cognition itself was conscripted into war.

Across radar, penicillin, highways, and codebreaking runs a common thread: the suspension of peacetime rules. Feasibility, cost, and long-term consequences yield to the logic of survival. This should not be mistaken for romance. Desperation fosters speed, but also fragility; what is born under fire is not always built to last. Yet it reveals an enduring truth: entrenched systems rarely change without duress. Crisis functions as a peculiar permission slip—sanctioning what was once unthinkable.

There is a human analogue to this. Soldiers in memoirs recount discovering abilities they never imagined—improvising under pressure, redefining themselves in real time. Psychological innovation, if you will, emerges when the structures of identity collapse. The most decisive actions often come not from adherence to training manuals, but from spontaneous strategies forged in the crucible of uncertainty.

This invites a deeper question: must we always wait for catastrophe to break free of inertia? Could we, in theory, simulate the galvanising effects of crisis without enduring its destruction? These are not idle musings. They strike at the core of how societies think about reform and creativity. If bureaucracy is indeed the enemy of invention, how do we ignite progress without the spark of disaster?

History offers a sobering answer: the potential for ingenuity is embedded in human systems, but is too often smothered by habit and hierarchy. War, for all its horrors, has a brutal knack for stripping these away—forcing collaboration, dismantling assumptions, and revealing new possibilities. The paradox is cruel yet clear: some of the most fertile grounds for imagination are also the most perilous.

What follows is not a celebration but an inquiry into that paradox. From radar scopes to neural networks, battlefield improvisation to algorithmic warfare, the aim is to trace how necessity redraws the boundaries of the possible. The inventions of wartime do not merely close conflicts; they redefine the peace that follows. To understand their genesis is to glimpse how we might navigate the future—under pressure, without precedent, and perhaps, inevitably, with the heat of fire at our backs.

Invention in the Inferno

War compresses time and expands necessity. It extinguishes luxury and incubates innovation—not gently, but violently. The Second World War, the most expansive and mechanised conflict in human history, was also a paradoxical crucible of creativity. It did not nurture invention through foresight or idealism. It demanded it, under duress, in blood, and at speed. The question worth asking is not simply *what* was invented during this inferno, but *how*—and what that process tells us about the deeper mechanics of creativity under existential threat.

Radar, antibiotics, and the jet engine each illustrate a principle that often goes unnoticed in peacetime innovation: the removal of optionality. In contexts where time is abundant, invention is typically methodical, encumbered by protocols, budgets, and incremental testing. Wartime eliminates those constraints. When the Luftwaffe darkened British skies, and when the Wehrmacht rolled across Europe, the calculus changed. A delayed decision no longer risked economic inefficiency; it risked annihilation. Radar was not invented from a place of technical curiosity. It was wrenched from the abstract into the real because defeat was unthinkable.

The origins of radar trace back to the interwar years, when British scientists began experimenting with radio waves as a method of aircraft detection. But it was only the prospect of imminent invasion that turned theory into hardware. The work of Robert Watson-Watt and his team at Bawdsey Manor accelerated rapidly in 1935, leading to the Chain Home radar system that formed the backbone of Britain's air defence during the Battle of Britain. The underlying science predated the war. What the war provided was *clarity of priority* and an institutional tolerance for risk. The normal hesitations—scientific peer review, interdepartmental turf battles, commercial rivalries—were suspended. Wartime does not abolish bureaucracy, but it *inverts* it. The central question becomes not whether something is perfectly proven, but whether it is *possibly useful.*

A similar pattern is evident in the rise of antibiotics. Alexander Fleming discovered penicillin in 1928, but for over a decade it remained little more than an academic curiosity. It wasn't until the war that governments, recognising the astronomical toll of battlefield infections, threw their weight behind mass production. Howard Florey and Ernst Chain, working at the University of Oxford, succeeded in purifying and stabilising the compound. But the real breakthrough came not in the lab, but in the logistical apparatus of war. American pharmaceutical firms, enlisted under wartime contracts, pioneered methods for industrial-scale fermentation. Within a few years, penicillin availability had transformed combat medicine—slashing mortality rates and changing public expectations about the survivability of injury. War did not invent penicillin, but it imposed a timeline that peace had never justified.

This theme—*compressed timelines triggering exponential leaps*—finds perhaps its most dramatic expression in aviation. The jet engine, long theorised and sporadically prototyped in the 1930s, was refined under the shadow of war. Britain's Frank Whittle and Germany's Hans von Ohain, working independently, both developed functioning turbojet engines by the early 1940s. What had previously been dismissed as a futurist dream suddenly became an imperative. Speed, altitude, and range had become decisive variables. Dogfights over Europe and the Pacific were no longer just contests of piloting skill—they were tests of propulsion science. The jet engine was not the product of calm strategic planning. It was an act of desperation made manifest through engineering. The enemy's capability became the benchmark of one's own innovation. Creativity, in this context, was neither romantic nor self-directed. It was reactive, rivalrous, and immediate.

But invention in wartime is not only about tools and technologies. It is also about *conceptual agility*—the willingness to discard frameworks that no longer fit. Take the notion of centralised command. In theatres like North Africa and the Pacific, the rigidity of traditional top-down control structures proved inadequate for fast-moving, dispersed, and information-scarce battlefields. The necessity for decentralised decision-making—what would later be termed "mission command"—emerged not as a theoretical shift, but as a pragmatic adaptation. Junior officers had to be trusted to act on intent, not micromanaged plans. This was not taught in academies; it was learned in combat, often at staggering cost. The lesson here is psychological: that innovation often requires not just new devices, but *new permissions.*

Some of the most profound wartime innovations were not products of advanced science, but of constraint. The German V-2 rocket was technologically audacious, but its production relied heavily on forced labour from concentration camps—an ethical abomination that underscores how war can unmoor invention from morality. Meanwhile, the Soviet Union's use of camouflage, deception, and disinformation during the Battle of Kursk demonstrated that innovation could be cultural and cognitive, not just technical. These were strategies honed through hardship, not conceived in theory. The creative edge often belonged to those who could *adapt the fastest*, not those with the most resources.

The nature of innovation in wartime also blurs the distinction between destruction and design. The firebombing of cities like Dresden and Tokyo produced post-war urban environments radically different from those that preceded them—not by design, but as a side effect of devastation. Reconstruction, in many instances, had to begin from scratch. The necessity to rebuild enabled new architectural visions, new infrastructural systems, and even new modes of citizenship. In this way, war becomes a kind of uninvited architect. The bombs tear down the old order, but in doing so create the spatial and institutional voids into which novel ideas can flow. Whether those ideas are humane or authoritarian depends on who seizes the moment.

This leads to an unsettling insight: *destruction is often the precondition for creativity*. When existing systems are too entrenched to change from within, only external shocks—war, collapse, revolution—can clear the ground for renewal. This is not to glorify violence, but to recognise a brutal psychological pattern: that humans are often more responsive to loss than to possibility. The status quo does not yield to argument. It yields to trauma. This, perhaps, is the most tragic paradox of wartime invention. We are at our most innovative precisely when our continuity is most threatened.

Even within the horror, there are lessons. The culture of innovation that emerged during WWII laid the foundations for the post-war scientific boom: nuclear energy, space exploration, digital computing, and systems engineering all trace their roots to military necessity. But they also reveal the limits of foresight. Almost none of the transformative applications of these wartime inventions—whether commercial aviation, the internet, or mRNA technology—were anticipated by their originators. The conditions of war *accelerated* innovation, but they did not *control* it. What emerged was not a tightly managed portfolio of outcomes, but an unpredictable cascade of possibilities. War, in this sense, is a poor planner but an excellent disruptor.

So what does creativity under existential threat actually look like? It is not elegant. It is rarely optimal. It does not emerge from comfort or consensus. It thrives in the margins—among people and institutions willing to break rank, cross disciplines, and tolerate ambiguity. It is resourceful, irreverent, and often unsanctioned. Wartime creativity does not ask for permission. It asks what works. And when it finds something that does, it builds quickly and repurposes ruthlessly.

For modern societies, the implications are profound. If we know that high-stakes pressure can unlock dormant capabilities—both institutional and individual—then how can we simulate those conditions without invoking catastrophe? Can we design for urgency without actual peril? Or are we condemned to learn, again and again, only through fire?

History suggests that crisis is our most reliable accelerant. But the uncomfortable truth is that creativity, when unmoored from regulation and ego, can flourish just as violently as the conflicts that gave it birth. The real challenge is not in creating under fire—it is in sustaining that creativity when the fires go out. That is where civilisation is either remade—or merely relieved.

The Accidental Architect: War's Role in Shaping the Modern World

Wars destroy cities. They dismantle trade. They erase lives, redraw borders, and destabilise governments. But what they also do—more quietly, yet no less significantly—is build. Not deliberately, not always ethically, and almost never predictably, but decisively. Throughout modern history, war has functioned as an accidental architect, giving rise to some of the most fundamental systems that now underpin global society. From highways to the internet, from satellite communication to mass-production logistics, many of the infrastructures we rely on today were conceived not in boardrooms or universities, but in military operations rooms, airfields, and bunkers. The destruction of war, paradoxically, often leaves behind the scaffolding of new worlds.

Take, for instance, the interstate highway system in the United States. While commonly associated with President Dwight D. Eisenhower's 1956 Federal-Aid Highway Act, its roots stretch back to his experience in World War II. Eisenhower had been deeply impressed by Germany's Autobahn network—an innovation initially developed under the Nazi regime for rapid military transport. The strategic value of being able to move troops, weapons, and supplies across great distances at speed was not lost on him. Back in the United States, the absence of a similar system was not just inconvenient—it was a vulnerability. Thus, what would become one of the most significant civil engineering projects in human history emerged not from a desire for economic efficiency or domestic convenience, but from a doctrinal imperative: to protect the nation in the event of nuclear war or invasion.

This repurposing of military insight into civilian infrastructure is not an isolated incident. During the Second World War, the logistical demands of global warfare forced both Axis and Allied powers to refine supply chain management, standardise parts, and develop sophisticated maintenance protocols for vehicles, aircraft, and ships. The sheer scale of war logistics—moving millions of people and tonnes of equipment across continents—required innovations in inventory tracking, distribution, and redundancy planning. What began as a necessity on the battlefield soon migrated to the factory floor. The post-war boom in global shipping, commercial aviation, and multinational production networks owes much to this wartime inheritance. Without intending to, war created blueprints for industrial and infrastructural modernity.

One of the most transformative examples of war's architectural legacy is the internet. Its forerunner, ARPANET, was developed in the late 1960s by the United States Department of Defense. The Cold War context is critical: fearing that a Soviet nuclear attack could knock out communication hubs, American military strategists sought a decentralised network capable of surviving partial destruction. The resulting innovation—packet switching—allowed messages to be broken into small units and reassembled across distributed nodes. Though the original intent was military resilience, the architecture proved astonishingly versatile. By the 1990s, it had been co-opted for academic, commercial, and eventually public use. What had begun as a solution to the problem of annihilation became the foundation of a new kind of global civilisation.

The internet's origin story is a case study in how war does not merely destroy—it displaces problems. It forces a reevaluation of what matters most, and accelerates the evolution of systems that, once proven in crisis, become indispensable in peace. The protocols and patterns forged in wartime are rarely designed for elegance. They are built to function under stress, to outlast sabotage, and to adapt quickly. And yet, once tested, they often outperform their more deliberate peacetime counterparts. In this sense, war is less an inventor than an enabler. It strips away the constraints of consensus, forcing actions that would otherwise be bogged down in caution, politics, or ideology.

Nowhere is this clearer than in the Cold War's influence on technological infrastructure. The space race, born out of geopolitical rivalry between the United States and the Soviet Union, yielded not just a handful of moon landings, but a cascade of breakthroughs in satellite communication, weather forecasting, and materials science. GPS, another military innovation, was originally developed to improve the accuracy of missile guidance systems. Today, it underpins everything from aviation and agriculture to ride-sharing and logistics. The irony is striking: technologies created to target now serve to connect.

Yet the architectural legacy of war is not just technical—it is ideological and institutional. During the Second World War, the Allied powers developed integrated command structures, cross-border intelligence-sharing protocols, and multinational coordination mechanisms that would later inform institutions like NATO and the United Nations. These were not idealistic initiatives born of post-war diplomacy; they were logistical and strategic necessities, forged during the chaos of conflict. War forced cooperation before cooperation became policy. What emerged were the bones of international order, constructed not in the spirit of utopia, but under the pressure of mutual survival.

Even within the devastated landscapes of post-war Europe and Asia, we find instances where destruction became the precondition for architectural and institutional rebirth. West Germany's Autobahn was expanded, repurposed, and integrated into a national reconstruction plan that included housing, telecommunications, and manufacturing hubs. Japan's high-speed rail network, the Shinkansen, emerged in part from the ambition to rebuild and reimagine mobility after the war's total infrastructural collapse. These were not mere restorations—they were leaps forward. The tabula rasa created by bombing campaigns allowed for radical rethinking, sometimes with astonishing results. The cities that rose were not replicas of what had been lost; they were prototypes of what could be built.

This does not mean that war is a necessary condition for progress—far from it. But it is one of the few circumstances in which entrenched systems are suspended. Hierarchies collapse, funding restrictions are waived, experimental ideas are trialled because there is no alternative. In this strange vacuum of peacetime protocol, innovation can flourish—not because war is wise, but because it is unrelenting. The lesson for peacetime societies is uncomfortable: *our biggest breakthroughs often emerge when we stop demanding perfection and start tolerating failure at speed.*

There is also a psychological dimension to war's architectural influence. Military planners must think in terms of contingency, redundancy, and unpredictability. These habits of mind—often dismissed as overly cautious or pessimistic in civilian contexts—have proven indispensable in areas like cyber-security, climate adaptation, and crisis response. The mental infrastructure of strategic thinking, developed to navigate existential threat, has found its way into everything from urban planning to corporate risk management. Again, the transfer is indirect but potent. War reshapes not only our physical environments, but our cognitive frameworks.

Of course, the legacy is not uniformly positive. The militarisation of technology can hardwire authoritarian possibilities into the architecture of daily life. Surveillance systems pioneered for battlefield awareness now monitor civilian populations. Facial recognition software, drone technologies, and biometric databases—all with military pedigrees—have been redeployed in ways that raise profound ethical questions. The same logistical sophistication that feeds global commerce can also enable mass detentions, forced migrations, and supply chain manipulation in authoritarian regimes. War may be an architect, but it is not a benevolent one. It builds with indifference to long-term consequences.

This ambiguity is essential. To study the infrastructural legacy of war is not to celebrate conflict, but to recognise its catalytic role in shaping the systems we now take for granted. Many of the devices, networks, and policies that define modern life were not designed for us—they were adapted for us. They carry the fingerprints of strategists, not citizens; of generals, not visionaries. And yet, they have become ours to use, to question, and to reconfigure.

If war is an accidental architect, then we, as beneficiaries of its unintended legacies, must act as deliberate renovators. We inherit systems built for urgency, but we live in a world that demands sustainability. We operate networks born from paranoia, in societies that claim to value openness. To reconcile these contradictions is not to erase history, but to understand its structure—and to build, at last, with intent.

Codebreakers and the Birth of the Digital Mind

It is one of the grand ironies of the twentieth century that modern computation—the backbone of nearly every system in contemporary life—was not born in a laboratory seeking progress, but in a mansion turned military base trying to stop annihilation. Bletchley Park, an unassuming country house in Buckinghamshire, became the unlikely crucible for a revolution that would change not only the outcome of the Second World War but also the future of human intelligence. At the centre of this unlikely epic was Alan Turing: mathematician, cryptanalyst, and often misunderstood genius whose conceptualisation of the universal computing machine laid the theoretical foundation for today's digital world. In the context of existential warfare, what began as a race to decode enemy transmissions evolved into the earliest expressions of machine logic, artificial thought, and algorithmic power.

The war demanded more than manpower and munitions; it required the industrialisation of thought. German military communications, encrypted through the Enigma machine, posed a strategic nightmare for the Allies. The complexity of the cipher—rooted in a system of rotating rotors and plugboard permutations—rendered traditional decryption methods functionally obsolete. Each day's new settings meant that a brute-force approach was virtually impossible within the timeframe intelligence was needed. Human intuition alone could not meet the scale of the problem. What was needed was not faster hands, but faster logic. In response, Turing proposed a radical idea: build a machine capable of simulating logical operations faster than any human team. The result, the Bombe, was a proto-computational device designed to exploit the structural redundancies of language and mechanical settings to isolate probable keys. The breakthrough was not simply mechanical—it was conceptual. Turing and his colleagues were not just breaking codes; they were building a new architecture of cognition.

This shift—towards the mechanisation of reasoning—was arguably more significant than the content of the messages themselves. For the first time, machines were being designed to execute abstract logical functions, effectively mimicking certain forms of human problem-solving. This was not automation in the industrial sense, where machines replicate physical labour. It was a form of cognitive outsourcing—offloading the labour of inference, analysis, and recognition to an engineered system. The implications, though scarcely understood at the time, were seismic. Turing's wartime models directly anticipated the logic circuits of later computers, and his 1936 paper "On Computable Numbers" remains a cornerstone of computational theory. Yet it was the war that moved these ideas from speculation to necessity. *Crisis became catalyst.*

The structure of the Bletchley effort also presaged features of modern digital environments: interdisciplinarity, secrecy, and modularity. Linguists, chess players, mathematicians, engineers, and crossword enthusiasts worked side-by-side, each contributing fragments of expertise. This model—of distributed cognition, broken down into solvable parts and reassembled into insight—mirrors how modern artificial intelligence systems are built today. No one person can claim full authorship of a neural network or data architecture; the task is too complex, the layers too interdependent. What Bletchley pioneered was a blueprint for how intelligent systems—both human and artificial—might be constructed, maintained, and optimised under extreme constraint.

But the historical legacy of Bletchley Park is not just technical. It is deeply philosophical. The idea that thought could be reduced to a series of operations, and that those operations could be implemented mechanically, challenged centuries of assumptions about human uniqueness. If code could simulate choice, inference, and even prediction, then what distinguished the mind from the machine? This ontological rupture—silent but profound—set the stage for debates that persist today around artificial intelligence, machine autonomy, and algorithmic ethics.

We see echoes of this rupture in today's technology landscapes. AI systems built on machine learning principles—descendants, in a conceptual sense, of Turing's vision—now drive decisions in finance, security, healthcare, and governance. But as these systems grow more powerful, the philosophical tension deepens: what do we lose when cognition becomes computation? Turing's post-war work, particularly his famous Turing Test, posed the problem directly—how would we recognise machine intelligence if it behaved indistinguishably from human intelligence? The deeper question he gestured towards remains unsettled: *what are the ethical responsibilities of creators when intelligence becomes engineered?*

The surveillance implications are particularly salient. Much of today's algorithmic infrastructure traces back to wartime precedents in code-breaking, interception, and signal intelligence. The difference is one of scope and scale. Where Bletchley Park focused on decrypting enemy transmissions, modern surveillance systems often operate on domestic populations, harvesting data in real-time, pre-emptively analysing behaviour, and classifying identities. The line between protection and intrusion is blurred, and often redrawn not by public consensus, but by technological capability. That this apparatus evolved from wartime imperatives is crucial. The logic of the battlefield—anticipate threat, eliminate uncertainty, act pre-emptively—has quietly colonised the logic of everyday governance.

Indeed, one of the great paradoxes of the digital age is that its liberating potential—instant communication, distributed knowledge, decentralised platforms—sits atop an architecture born of secrecy and control. The very protocols that enable connectivity were developed to manage isolation and mitigate risk. The ethic of openness now depends on systems designed for containment. This dual legacy is neither accidental nor easily untangled. It demands that we confront a question posed implicitly by Turing's generation: *can tools built for conflict be repurposed for cohesion, or will their original logic persist beneath the surface?*

There is no simple answer. But history suggests that awareness is the first condition of ethical reconfiguration. At Bletchley Park, intelligence was centralised, classified, and guarded with obsessive discipline. Today's data landscapes operate with similar opacity—proprietary algorithms, surveillance agreements, and digital infrastructure governed by unaccountable private actors. Yet the stakes have grown exponentially. Where Turing's machines sought patterns in enemy encryption, today's algorithms seek patterns in human life—preferences, movements, social connections, cognitive habits. *The enemy, it turns out, is no longer foreign. It is us, modelled as data.*

This realisation makes Turing's life story all the more tragic and prescient. Persecuted for his homosexuality despite his pivotal wartime contributions, Turing died in 1954, officially ruled a suicide. That the architect of digital intelligence was destroyed by the social ignorance of his time is a bitter reminder of the chasm between technological progress and moral clarity. His story underscores a recurring truth: *systems may evolve faster than societies.* The capacity to compute does not guarantee the capacity to comprehend what that power entails—or how it should be wielded.

Today, as AI systems begin to demonstrate forms of generative language, autonomous learning, and strategic reasoning, the ghost of Bletchley returns. The questions that Turing posed in the context of wartime code-breaking are no longer theoretical. Can intelligence be programmed without conscience? Can logic operate ethically in the absence of empathy? Can systems designed for efficiency accommodate ambiguity, contradiction, and moral weight?

If the digital mind was born in war, then its future must be governed in peace. This means more than just regulating technology. It means cultivating an intellectual culture that remembers its origins—where abstraction was wielded not for profit, but for survival; where secrecy was necessary, but not natural; where innovation was urgent, but bounded by human cost. To study Bletchley Park is not only to trace the genesis of computers. It is to encounter a moment when intelligence was recalibrated—compressed, encoded, and, finally, externalised.

What remains is the responsibility of interpretation. The machines that emerged from Turing's vision do not understand the meaning of the patterns they process. That burden falls to us. Whether we use them to decrypt the past, govern the present, or design the future depends not on their capacity, but on our clarity. We do not lack intelligence. We risk lacking reflection.

Necessity and the Unwritten Rulebook

History often lionises innovators as visionaries—men and women with foresight, strategy, and singular genius. But war offers a different profile of the innovator: someone who acts not from calm foresight but from the edge of collapse. Under the relentless pressure of crisis, when institutional rules falter and doctrinal scaffolding gives way, what remains is necessity. And from necessity emerges not planned invention, but raw improvisation—an innovation born not of privilege or luxury, but of urgent adaptation. This is the innovation that writes no manifestos and makes no speeches. It leaves no time for consensus. It thrives in disruption. And often, it rewires the innovator in the process.

During moments of profound breakdown—when command structures implode, when terrain becomes unpredictable, when supply chains are severed—commanders and combatants alike find themselves untethered from the rulebooks that once defined their operational world. Yet history shows that these are precisely the conditions in which paradigm shifts occur. Take the British evacuation at Dunkirk in 1940. The retreat was a military failure on conventional terms, but the ad hoc mobilisation of hundreds of civilian vessels—fishing boats, pleasure craft, merchant ships—redefined the logic of logistics. Desperation overrode doctrine. Naval protocol was subordinated to emotional necessity. In doing so, a mythic narrative of resilience was forged, but so too was a practical shift in how states perceived civil-military interoperability.

What Dunkirk demonstrates is that *when the formal playbook collapses, the informal imagination expands*. And this holds true not only for material systems but for the cognitive frameworks through which actors interpret their world. In psychological terms, crisis is a form of forced deconstruction. Established patterns of reasoning, belief, and perception are destabilised. Under extreme pressure, the mind abandons hierarchies it once trusted and seeks new mental shortcuts, often fusing intuition with fragments of experience. The result is what might be called *psychological innovation*: a spontaneous reorganisation of mental models under duress.

Consider the case of the Battle of Stalingrad. Soviet commanders, outnumbered and encircled, restructured their entire tactical posture around urban combat—something previously marginal in Soviet military doctrine. Buildings were turned into vertical kill zones, with defenders exploiting stairwells and basements to turn height into hazard. In the psychological environment of street fighting, where every window might host a sniper and every sewer a flanking route, situational awareness mutated. Soldiers began processing space in three-dimensional tactical terms, radically different from open-field manoeuvres. The transformation was not only tactical but cognitive. Standard planning had to be replaced by hyper-local decision-making, sensory overload managed by what modern neuroscience would classify as *cognitive compression*: the ability to suppress irrelevant data and hyperfocus on immediate cues. Necessity didn't just rewrite the map; it rewired the mind navigating it.

At a broader scale, military institutions have long used peacetime to codify doctrine, build predictable systems, and create repeatable models. But the rhythms of real war almost always dismantle these structures. The Vietnam War's counterinsurgency campaigns, for example, revealed the irrelevance of traditional metrics of success—territory held, body counts, supply lines—to conflicts rooted in ideology, terrain intimacy, and civilian enmeshment. US commanders, facing an elusive enemy and deteriorating morale, began experimenting with civic outreach programmes, psychological operations, and decentralised unit autonomy. Many of these ideas were initially seen as unorthodox, even subversive. But the inability of conventional firepower to secure victory forced a reckoning with operational assumptions. Out of failure came the seeds of future doctrine—though not always recognised in time to change the war's trajectory.

What links these disparate examples is the tension between formal design and emergent necessity. Conventional strategic planning rests on assumptions of predictability, rational actors, and linear escalation. But warfare, as chaos theorists remind us, operates more like a complex adaptive system—non-linear, interdependent, and sensitive to minor variables. When a tank breaks down in an unexpected location, or when a message is intercepted or mistranslated, cascading consequences unfold that no blueprint could anticipate. In these moments, rules are not merely bent—they are discarded, because the system no longer supports them. This is not an admission of chaos, but a recognition of *creative disorder.*

And it is not limited to commanders and generals. Individual soldiers, medics, engineers, and civilians are often forced to innovate not out of desire, but out of a collapsing environment that leaves no other option. A well-documented case is the improvisation of battlefield surgery protocols in the Pacific Theatre of WWII. Lacking proper equipment and faced with mass casualties, medics developed techniques for triage, tourniquet design, and rapid haemorrhage control that later influenced civilian trauma medicine. Innovation here was not an epiphany—it was a reaction to catastrophe, distilled into practice under constraint.

Perhaps most revealing is how personal identity shifts alongside institutional collapse. War memoirs frequently reveal that individual transformation accelerates in inverse proportion to structural reliability. In other words, *when systems fail, selves are rebuilt.* One former Royal Marine who served in Helmand Province described how the loss of radio contact during a firefight triggered a form of temporal dissociation—what psychologists term a 'perceptual bubble'—in which time, decision, and self-narration collapsed into moment-to-moment survival. But in the aftermath, that same soldier reported a radical shift in moral perspective: a heightened sensitivity to consequence, a suspicion of command assumptions, and a greater tolerance for ambiguity. The psychic trauma was real. But so too was the transformation of mental frameworks, a kind of evolution under fire.

This introduces an uncomfortable truth: some of the most effective forms of human learning occur under conditions of duress. The mind, when faced with contradiction, danger, or uncertainty, sheds what is non-functional. This process is not always neat. Nor is it always positive. But it is potent. And it has implications well beyond the battlefield. Post-war periods often become incubators of civilian innovation, precisely because returning veterans bring with them not just trauma, but unorthodox thinking. Their exposure to failure, improvisation, and the collapse of normalcy enables them to challenge assumptions that peace has allowed to ossify.

From Silicon Valley founders with military pasts to emergency response planners drawing on asymmetric warfare models, the traces of psychological innovation—born in collapse—reverberate across sectors. These are not always celebrated, because they do not fit traditional narratives of heroism or design. They are ambiguous, fragile, even ethically murky. But they are real. And they challenge the idea that innovation is always a product of deliberate planning. Sometimes, it is the absence of planning—its breakdown, its insufficiency—that reveals what human ingenuity is truly capable of.

To understand innovation under these conditions is to discard the myth of control. It is to recognise that systems, however sophisticated, are not ends in themselves but scaffolds—and that when the scaffolds fall, the mind builds differently. Not better. Not worse. Just differently. More flexibly. More responsively. And often, more honestly.

The unwritten rulebook is not a theory; it is an observation. That when people are stripped of certainty, what emerges is not necessarily chaos, but recalibration. Not abandonment of purpose, but redefinition of method. This is as true in combat as it is in collapse, as relevant to institutions as it is to individuals. And it is why war, despite its horror, continues to reveal something profound:

not just what humans can destroy, but how they rebuild under impossible conditions—and in doing so, redraw the boundaries of the possible.

Chapter 4
The Civilian Front: War as a Social Earthquake

Wars are often recounted in the familiar language of campaigns, treaties, and shifting alliances. Yet behind the maps and communiqués lies another narrative—slower, quieter, but no less decisive. This is the story of societies under strain, of what happens when conflict reaches beyond the battlefield and presses its weight upon the fabric of everyday life. War does not merely carve new borders or rearrange political hierarchies; it unsettles identities, upends long-held norms, and brings dormant tensions roaring to the surface. It is fought not only in trenches or war rooms but also in the workshop, the schoolyard, the backstreet, and the artist's studio—the civilian front, where the shockwaves of conflict jolt loose the foundations on which a culture rests. Rarely does the end of fighting mean a simple return to what came before. More often, something different emerges—conceived in hardship, altered in ways that cannot be undone.

This chapter follows those deeper social tremors, tracing how the collapse of established orders can ignite radical reconfigurations of public life. But it resists the temptation to drape such change in easy optimism. Upheaval born of catastrophe is not inherently progress. It can be contradictory, uneven, and fought over in ways that leave as many fractures as they mend. And yet it reveals much. It lays bare the scaffolding of civic life—gender hierarchies, shared values, the very idea of collective identity—and compels a reassessment of what a society believes, how it organises itself, and who is counted as part of its "we."

Few shifts are as visible, or as contested, as the wartime remaking of gender roles. Images of women in boiler suits and factory yards—welding, riveting, filling shells—have become cultural shorthand for the Second World War, but the scale of that transformation is often underestimated. In the United States, in Britain, across the Soviet Union, the mass enlistment of women into industry was not just a logistical fix; it was a live experiment in social malleability. Laws and customs that had seemed immovable gave way under the pressure of survival, exposing how elastic "traditional" gender arrangements really were. The aftermath told its own tale. In some countries, women were briskly channelled back into domesticity, their wartime roles treated as an aberration. In others, the shift was absorbed into law and cultural expectation. The divergence leaves a lingering question: when does an emergency adjustment harden into reform? And whose decision is that to make?

This phenomenon is far from confined to industrial powers. In recent years, the Kurdish Women's Protection Units (YPJ) in northern Syria have defied both local patriarchal norms and the global military imagination. Born partly from the existential threat of ISIS, the YPJ wove armed defence together with a feminist ideology that treats women's liberation as the very core of the struggle. The sight of women in combat fatigues, rifle in hand, in a region long defined by male martial dominance, does more than challenge stereotypes—it forces a harder inquiry into the nature of agency under siege. Is a woman's weapon an emblem of liberation, or a symbol of tragic necessity? Perhaps, inevitably, it is both.

The redefinition of identity during war is not restricted to gender. Conflict often compels entire populations to renegotiate what it means to be a citizen. Post-genocide Rwanda offers a stark example: after 1994, rebuilding meant more than repairing roads and buildings. It required reshaping the national self—determining who belonged, who could speak, who could teach. Education became both a practical necessity and a political minefield. Curricula were rebuilt to promote reconciliation, critical inquiry, and honest engagement with history. Yet this came with wrenching dilemmas: how do you teach a past in which neighbours became killers? How do you create a shared narrative when the very idea of "shared" has been broken?

Japan, in the years after its imperial defeat, faced similar trials in its classrooms. Schoolbooks were repeatedly rewritten as governments veered between contrition, defensiveness, and attempts at reinvention. Some softened uncomfortable facts; others confronted them outright, risking public outrage. The process underscored a truth too easily overlooked: education is not just policy. It is a moral battleground, especially in the wake of war.

Resistance movements further reveal how deeply war penetrates civilian consciousness. The German White Rose group—students armed only with typewriters, leaflets, and moral conviction—mounted an intellectual rebellion against the Nazi state. Their campaign, though small and swiftly crushed, demonstrated a form of courage measured not in military victories but in the refusal to submit to falsehood. For this, they were executed. Their brief defiance still prompts uneasy questions: what does it mean to resist when success is implausible? What sustains one's resolve when solidarity is scarce?

Afghanistan's long modern history offers a more sprawling, improvisational resistance. Across decades of Soviet occupation, Taliban rule, and foreign intervention, Afghans have resisted in ways both armed and subtle—through fighters in the hills, clandestine schools for girls, secretive journalists, even the quiet preservation of art and heritage. Such acts blur the line between survival and idealism, between practicality and protest. They suggest that prolonged conflict can breed a mental agility, a capacity to hold contradictions in tension and adapt to shifting moral terrain. This flexibility is not tidy, nor always admirable—but it can be the only possible way to endure.

Art, too, becomes a means of navigation through the wreckage. The Harlem Renaissance, while not born solely from war, was shaped by the dislocations of World War I and the Great Migration, transforming loss and displacement into music, verse, and new aesthetic visions. It asserted identity in the teeth of systemic erasure. In Europe, the absurdist provocations of Dada erupted from the absurdity of the Great War itself, mocking the rationalism that had led to mechanised slaughter. Its apparent nonsense was, in truth, a scalpel—cutting into the madness beneath the order.

Post-war Japan saw artists like Kurosawa Akira and writers such as Kenzaburō Ōe wrestling with the aftermath of atomic devastation and imperial collapse. Their work did not simply mourn; it interrogated. They asked how a society could carry the knowledge of having been both oppressor and victim, and whether art could excavate a truth deeper than propaganda or denial. These films, novels, and plays were more than cultural products—they were arguments: about memory, dignity, guilt, and the possibilities of moral renewal.

Across all these cases—the factories and classrooms, the underground presses and guerrilla studios—war is not only destruction. It is exposure. It reveals the deepest priorities of a people: what they will preserve, abandon, or reimagine. And it challenges the easy framing of civilians as mere bystanders. In their responses, they become co-authors of the future. The formal front lines may shift, but the stakes remain embedded in homes, institutions, and cultural memory.

War, then, should be read not solely as the clash of armies, but as a social earthquake—cracking open the ground beneath norms and identities, scattering the familiar, and leaving behind both rubble and new foundations. The questions it poses are as urgent as they are uncomfortable: Who joins in the reconstruction? Which beliefs are buried, revived, or recast? Whose voices ring loudest, and whose fade into silence?

To grapple with these is not to diminish the suffering that war brings, but to admit its complexity. Amid the ruin, something else often begins—fragile, improvised, yet stubbornly human. A recalibration of how to live together, how to remember, how to resist, and, in time, how to rebuild.

The Shifting Role of Women in Wartime:

The transformation of warfare has always been entwined with the transformation of labour, identity, and power. Yet perhaps no shift is as consequential—or as under-analysed—as the changing role of women in wartime. Not as mere auxiliaries, nor symbolic figures of sacrifice or stoic motherhood, but as agents of industrial might, political resistance, combat innovation, and post-war social restructuring. War does not simply "invite" women into the public sphere; it forcibly repositions them there, often irreversibly, by stripping away the ordinary scaffolding of gendered norms under the pressure of national survival. And in doing so, it raises the broader question: when structures collapse, who rebuilds them—and who decides the blueprint?

One of the most iconic images to emerge from the twentieth century is that of Rosie the Riveter—rolled sleeves, red bandana, and clenched fist beneath the slogan *We Can Do It!*. On the surface, it is a celebration of patriotic mobilisation during World War II. Beneath that surface, however, lies something more complex: a state-sanctioned reconfiguration of gendered labour. Between 1940 and 1945, over six million women entered the American workforce, occupying roles in munitions factories, shipyards, and aircraft production lines. These were not symbolic roles; they were structurally indispensable to the war effort. Yet the prevailing assumption at the time was that this mobilisation was temporary—a necessary deviation rather than a true transformation.

But history does not always obey the intentions of policymakers. Although post-war campaigns did, in many cases, encourage women to return to domesticity, the social contract had already shifted. Women's exposure to financial independence, industrial competence, and public visibility created a new reference point—one that could not be fully erased. The genie, once released, did not crawl back into the bottle. It lingered, reappearing in the form of feminist movements, civil rights struggles, and ongoing debates over economic equity. *Wartime labour, in this case, acted as both a rupture and a rehearsal.*

The phenomenon was not confined to the United States. In the Soviet Union, where existential threat was absolute, the integration of women into the military-industrial apparatus was even more expansive. Soviet women served not only as factory workers but as snipers, pilots, tank drivers, and partisans. The "Night Witches," a female bomber regiment, flew over 23,000 missions against the German army. Their presence wasn't framed as revolutionary but pragmatic—there was no one else left to fly. Yet pragmatism soon gave way to mythos, and then to political erasure. After the war, these women were often sidelined, their contributions diminished in official memory. What had been a moment of parity reverted to a form of selective amnesia. But the cultural memory, however faint, endured—whispered in memoirs, photographs, and informal networks of remembrance.

In more recent decades, this dynamic has re-emerged in radically different contexts. The Kurdish Women's Protection Units (YPJ), operating in northern Syria, represent one of the most striking contemporary cases of female military engagement. Here, women are not merely participating in war—they are redefining its logic. The YPJ blends armed resistance with an explicit ideological commitment to gender equality, rooted in the political philosophy of Abdullah Öcalan. Female fighters are not exceptions; they are the vanguard of a reimagined social order. This is not without contradiction. The use of weapons by women has been alternately celebrated and condemned, depending on the observer's lens. But the deeper question is structural: *Can gender equality emerge through war without replicating the very hierarchies it seeks to dismantle?* The YPJ is not a finished answer, but it is a compelling challenge to existing paradigms.

This pattern—of war acting as a gender disruptor—is echoed in less visible, but equally significant, domains. In post-conflict societies, women are often tasked with the double burden of reconstruction: not just rebuilding infrastructure, but reweaving the social fabric. This includes caregiving, educational reform, local governance, and even informal justice mechanisms in regions where formal institutions have collapsed. In Rwanda, women played an outsized role in post-genocide reconciliation, comprising nearly half of the parliament by the early 2000s—the highest proportion of any country at the time. This was not simply because of legal quotas or international pressure. It reflected a practical reality: the war had decimated the male population, and the surviving women had no choice but to lead. Out of necessity emerged a new form of legitimacy.

However, it would be naïve to interpret this solely as progress. Wartime openings for women are often conditional, contingent, and vulnerable to reversal. The inclusion of women during crisis does not guarantee emancipation. It can just as easily be instrumentalised—as seen in various propaganda campaigns that glorify female contribution while denying female autonomy. In Vietnam, for example, women fighters were celebrated in nationalist rhetoric but often denied real political agency in the post-war state. Similarly, in the Democratic Republic of Congo, women have served as peacebuilders and mediators even as they remain structurally excluded from formal negotiations. The line between empowerment and exploitation remains perilously thin.

What makes wartime gender shifts so revealing is their capacity to expose the elasticity of societal norms. Norms that once seemed immutable—women "naturally" belonging in the home, or men as default protectors—are suspended, retooled, or outright discarded under the weight of crisis. War, in this sense, operates as a stress test on the gender contract. It shows that roles are not ordained by biology or culture alone, but by a complex interplay of necessity, power, and narrative control.

This becomes particularly visible when examining post-war legal and institutional reforms. The British experience following both world wars illustrates this clearly. The Representation of the People Act of 1918, granting partial suffrage to women, was passed in direct response to their wartime contributions. Yet full suffrage did not arrive until a decade later, and gender wage equality remains elusive to this day. The lesson here is sobering: *recognition does not automatically translate into justice.* Institutional inertia often outlives the transformative energy of crisis. But the seed is planted. And once planted, it resists erasure.

At the cultural level, war also alters how femininity itself is coded. During the First World War, British nursing became a symbol of female patriotism and stoic sacrifice. In the Second World War, Hollywood films alternated between portraying women as virtuous mothers and seductive spies. These images were not trivial. They shaped public imagination and policy alike. By scripting what was deemed acceptable behaviour for women in wartime, they implicitly defined what was unacceptable. They marked the boundaries of moral legitimacy, with real consequences for those who transgressed.

It is also worth noting that the impact of war on women is not limited to those directly engaged in labour or combat. Civilian women in occupied territories, refugee camps, or conflict zones often undergo transformations that are harder to quantify but no less profound. The need to negotiate with occupying forces, protect children, procure food, or preserve cultural continuity—all these tasks require forms of leadership and innovation that rarely make it into history books. Yet they are foundational to survival. In such settings, power often becomes relational rather than positional. Authority is earned not through rank but through competence, credibility, and care. These are the hidden forms of agency that feminist scholars have increasingly sought to illuminate.

Ultimately, the shifting role of women in wartime is not a footnote to history—it is a central narrative. It is a story of contingency and resilience, of abrupt openings and painful retrenchments, of symbolic inclusion and strategic marginalisation. It forces us to re-examine how power is distributed, how legitimacy is conferred, and how agency is both granted and seized. More importantly, it reveals that the structures we take for granted are far more fluid than they appear.

Wartime, paradoxically, becomes a moment of both extreme constraint and unexpected possibility. It shatters certainties and imposes new logics. Whether these logics endure depends not only on post-war politics but on the narratives societies choose to tell themselves. Will women be remembered as temporary placeholders or as permanent co-authors of history? Will their sacrifices be sentimentalised or institutionalised? These are not merely academic questions. They shape the blueprint of the future. And they begin, often invisibly, on the civilian front.

Education in the Rubble:

When buildings collapse under bombs or machetes, and societies fracture along ethnic, ideological or religious lines, it is often the education system that must rise from the rubble not merely to instruct, but to reconstruct. In the wake of war or genocide, the classroom becomes more than a site of learning—it becomes a battleground for identity, legitimacy, memory and national redemption. The stakes are existential, the questions unforgiving: What kind of citizens should we produce now? What history should we teach, and whose version of it? And what purpose should education serve when survival—not success—has been the defining metric for an entire generation?

Rwanda, following the 1994 genocide, provides one of the clearest and most sobering examples. In just one hundred days, over 800,000 people were killed, and the nation's institutional fabric was left in ruins. Among the many systems paralysed, the education sector was especially hollowed out—not only physically, with schools destroyed or repurposed as sites of massacre, but morally. Teachers had participated in killings. Curricula had been used to entrench ethnic division. Education itself had, at times, served the machinery of genocide rather than shielding society from it. In this context, post-conflict reconstruction demanded not a simple reform, but a wholesale reimagining of what education should mean.

Rwanda's post-genocide educational reforms were not driven by abstract developmental goals; they were shaped by the immediate need to prevent the recurrence of mass violence. The government placed citizenship education, reconciliation, and unity at the heart of the national curriculum. Controversially, it abolished ethnic identifiers in official discourse—banning the public use of the terms Hutu and Tutsi in schools—and rewrote history textbooks to reflect a shared national narrative. Whether this approach fostered genuine reconciliation or imposed selective forgetting remains debated. But the underlying logic is clear: *education became the primary theatre in which the country's post-trauma identity was being negotiated.*

This pattern is not unique to Rwanda. Across post-war societies, education becomes a key mechanism for either continuity or rupture. After the Second World War, West Germany faced the formidable task of *Entnazifizierung*—denazification—not only of government and industry, but of the minds and memories of its youth. The education system, complicit under the Third Reich, had to be rebuilt under Allied supervision, with new textbooks, teacher retraining, and the introduction of democratic principles as core values. The goal was to create not only informed students, but immunised citizens—individuals capable of resisting authoritarianism. Yet progress was uneven and often met with societal resistance. For many Germans, confronting the recent past was painful, and denial or nostalgia often crept back into public discourse. Education, in this setting, functioned not as a panacea but as an ongoing site of ideological contestation.

What makes post-conflict education uniquely potent—and uniquely perilous—is the fact that it does not operate in a vacuum. The post-war classroom is embedded within a society still processing grief, anger, fear, and hope. Teachers are not neutral conduits of information; they are survivors, sometimes perpetrators, often both. Students do not enter the classroom as blank slates—they arrive bearing inherited trauma, whispered family narratives, and competing versions of truth. This makes the curriculum not just a pedagogical tool, but a political and psychological instrument. Every decision—what to teach, what to omit, how to frame the past—is loaded with implications for social cohesion or fragmentation.

South Africa's post-apartheid experience is illustrative. After 1994, the government introduced a curriculum aimed at building a "Rainbow Nation," rooted in democratic values, multiculturalism, and human rights. However, the very attempt to craft a unifying historical narrative was fraught. Some accused the new system of sanitising the brutality of apartheid; others argued it leaned too heavily into victimisation. Meanwhile, many teachers, themselves products of the apartheid regime, struggled to adapt to the new ethos. Here again, education became a mirror of unresolved tensions: *a space where ideals collided with lived contradictions*.

In some post-conflict societies, particularly where state institutions remain weak, educational innovation emerges from non-state actors. In post-war Liberia, for example, NGOs and community organisations often played a more agile and responsive role than the Ministry of Education. Trauma counselling was integrated into schools. Arts-based curricula—drama, storytelling, visual arts—were used to help children process violence and grief. This decentralised model fostered psychological healing in ways standardised systems often cannot. But it also introduced new challenges of coherence, quality control, and sustainability. Innovation in the rubble is often experimental by necessity, not by choice.

One of the most powerful tensions in post-war education reform lies between truth-telling and stability. Transitional justice mechanisms—such as truth commissions—often generate volumes of material on wartime atrocities. But how, and when, should these findings be incorporated into school curricula? In post-genocide Cambodia, for instance, it took decades before schools began teaching students about the Khmer Rouge period in any substantive way. Political sensitivities, generational divides, and elite interests delayed the integration of historical truth into formal education. The result was a collective amnesia in the public sphere, even as trauma persisted in private lives. Here, education was less a tool of reckoning than a strategy of deferral.

This raises a more fundamental question: *Should post-conflict education prioritise healing or accuracy?* These goals are not always aligned. Efforts to foster national unity can sometimes come at the cost of historical complexity. Simplified narratives may offer emotional clarity, but risk entrenching myths. Conversely, rigorous engagement with the past can destabilise fragile coalitions. Policymakers, educators, and communities must navigate this delicate terrain with care. There are no easy templates, only context-specific trade-offs.

It is also worth noting that educational reform is not just about content—it is about infrastructure, access, and equity. In Bosnia and Herzegovina, years after the Dayton Accords, children still attend "two schools under one roof," where Croat and Bosniak students share the same buildings but are taught different curricula in separate classrooms. This phenomenon, driven by ethnicised politics, perpetuates division even in peacetime. It reflects how *education systems can become both symptoms and sources of societal fragmentation*, especially when policy is captured by identity politics.

At the other end of the spectrum, education can serve as a rare point of unity. In post-earthquake Haiti, where political instability compounded social suffering, education initiatives were used as vehicles for civic renewal. International donors and local communities collaborated on curriculum reform, teacher training, and the rebuilding of schools. While results were uneven, the effort underscored a key insight: when formal institutions fail, education can serve as a substitute state—an anchor of normalcy, legitimacy, and future-oriented thinking.

This forward orientation is essential. Post-conflict education is not simply about repairing what was lost; it is about imagining what could be. It provides a generational bridge between the trauma of the past and the possibility of something better. This demands a particular kind of pedagogy—one that fosters critical thinking, ethical reasoning, and emotional resilience. It also demands humility. Post-war societies must resist the temptation to instrumentalise education for short-term gains. Instead, they must recognise it as a slow, complex, and deeply human process of rebuilding not just minds, but moral worlds.

One final point bears emphasising. Education in post-conflict settings is not merely a technical challenge—it is a philosophical one. It forces societies to ask: What kind of people do we want our children to become? What virtues should we prioritise—obedience or curiosity, loyalty or justice, conformity or courage? These are not just educational questions. They are existential ones, and their answers will shape the moral architecture of the post-war order.

The stakes could not be higher. In the absence of thoughtful, courageous educational reform, the cycle of violence often resumes. Resentments are passed down, wounds fester, and narratives of victimhood calcify into ideologies of vengeance. But where education is wielded with insight and integrity, it can interrupt these cycles. It can offer not just knowledge, but dignity. Not just skills, but solidarity. And not just history, but hope.

Resistance, Rebellion, and the Psychology of Occupation:

To resist is to remain human under conditions designed to erase that very possibility. Occupation is not merely the control of territory—it is the slow, relentless attempt to control thought, language, and moral instinct. Against this background, acts of rebellion—especially small, quiet ones—are not only political gestures but existential declarations. Whether it is a student leafleting against a regime, or a villager hiding a radio transmitter in a cave, resistance becomes less about outcome than about affirmation: a refusal to let fear or force have the final word.

One of the most enduring symbols of moral defiance in the face of authoritarianism is the White Rose movement in Nazi Germany. Founded by university students in Munich in 1942, including siblings Hans and Sophie Scholl, the White Rose group disseminated a series of leaflets condemning the Third Reich's crimes and calling for passive resistance. Their appeal was not framed in strategic or militaristic terms. It was a *moral summons*, grounded in philosophical and Christian ethics, urging Germans to awaken from their complicity. The leaflets cited Goethe, Schiller, and the Bible—not to cloak the message in literary grandeur, but to reassert a shared cultural conscience. In one passage, they wrote: "We will not be silent. We are your bad conscience." The group was arrested and executed in 1943, but their words endured, later becoming required reading in German schools. Their power lay not in what they changed, but in what they preserved: the clarity of ethical judgement amid institutionalised evil.

What makes such acts so psychologically potent is that they often emerge in contexts designed to extinguish autonomy. Under occupation, the mechanisms of control are not only physical—checkpoints, curfews, surveillance—but also cognitive. Occupied populations are pressured to adapt, normalise, and eventually internalise a version of the world that benefits their oppressors. Resistance, then, becomes a way of reclaiming narrative agency. Even when success is implausible, *to resist is to assert the capacity to choose*—a radical act under total domination.

The Afghan resistance against both Soviet and later Western military presence illustrates this in a radically different context. Here, resistance has often been framed through military or ideological lenses—an insurgency, a jihad, a guerrilla campaign. But beneath the geopolitical abstractions lies a more intimate form of rebellion: a tenacious psychological refusal to be colonised. Afghan history is replete with examples of local resistance movements that were less coordinated than persistent—villagers feeding fighters, students hiding banned books, poets smuggling verses across borders. These are not romanticised anecdotes. They reflect a deeper psychological truth: that dignity, once threatened, becomes a renewable source of defiance. The terrain of Afghanistan has often been called "unforgiving," but it is the human terrain—the habits of honour, memory, and ancestral pride—that has truly defied conquest.

Resistance takes many forms, not all of them overt. In occupied France during the Second World War, while the Resistance movement involved sabotage and intelligence gathering, it also included quieter subversions: false papers forged in kitchens, banned books read by candlelight, radio messages shared in whispers. Each act chipped away at the occupier's monopoly on truth. What united these gestures was not coordination but conscience. As historian Robert Gildea observed, "the line between collaboration and resistance was often drawn daily, in private." The psychology of occupation pressures people into what political theorist James C. Scott calls "public transcripts"—behaviours performed under duress—and "hidden transcripts"—the whispered truths that sustain inner freedom. Resistance, in this sense, is as much about the preservation of *interiority* as it is about external action.

This dynamic is especially evident in contexts where resistance is punished not only with death, but with erasure. During Argentina's Dirty War (1976–1983), the regime disappeared thousands, including students, journalists, and dissidents. In response, the Mothers of the Plaza de Mayo—a group of women whose children had vanished—began weekly marches in front of the presidential palace, holding signs with their children's names and photos. They wore white headscarves embroidered with the names of the disappeared. Their protest was silent, but its message was deafening: we will not forget. In a political landscape where memory was a threat, *to remember publicly was an act of rebellion.* Their resistance lay not in overthrowing power but in refusing its most insidious weapon: oblivion.

The psychology of resistance is distinct from the psychology of revolution. The latter seeks to replace a system; the former seeks to *retain a self.* This is why moral resistance often appears small and paradoxical. A Jewish teacher in a Polish ghetto risking his life to hold secret classes. A Palestinian artist spray-painting a wall with humour and irony. A dissident journalist using metaphor and allegory to skirt censors. These acts are not designed to win wars. They are designed to prevent *psychological occupation*—the capture of language, thought, and hope.

But resistance is never pure. It is always entangled in fear, compromise, and survival. Many resist not by fighting, but by refusing to celebrate, by maintaining a critical silence, by helping others survive. Others collaborate outwardly while sheltering rebels privately. These ambiguities complicate the moral landscape, but they do not dilute it. On the contrary, they underscore an essential insight: *resistance is often the art of doing what little one can, when one cannot do more.*

Moreover, resistance has generational echoes. It often outlives its originators. The legacy of the White Rose lives in German civic culture not because of immediate political impact, but because it modelled a kind of courage that transcends circumstances. Afghan resistance folklore serves not just as political memory, but as a cultural template for future action. When young Rwandans today participate in peace-building workshops or trauma-informed education, they draw—whether consciously or not—on traditions of endurance encoded into their community memory. Resistance becomes inheritance.

This inheritance is not without danger. Glorifying resistance can slip into fetishising victimhood or legitimising endless conflict. Not all who resist are virtuous, and not all resistance is ethical. The psychological frame must remain vigilant: *resistance is not merely the opposite of oppression; it must also be a moral answer to it.* This is why movements that couple dissent with dignity—non-violent action, civil disobedience, subversive art—retain a special moral force. They reveal that what is being defended is not just a cause, but a code of being.

Even more subtly, resistance reveals the fragility of imposed power. If domination must be continuously policed, censored, and enforced, it signals its own insecurity. Occupiers fear the leaflets more than the guns because leaflets travel invisibly—in minds, in conversations, in consciences. The White Rose was hunted not for its reach, but for its resonance. The same logic applies today. In tightly controlled digital autocracies, the meme, the whisper, the coded joke—these are the new samizdat. Their power lies not in overwhelming the state, but in illuminating its absurdity.

As technology evolves, so too do the tools of resistance. Encrypted messaging, anonymous blogs, decentralised networks—all offer new spaces for defiance. Yet the psychological constants remain. Resistance still begins with recognition: that something is wrong, that silence is complicity, that action—however small—is a form of authorship over one's moral fate. In this light, resistance is not the reserve of the heroic few. It is a distributed capacity, activated whenever conscience refuses to outsource its duty to circumstances.

Perhaps that is the enduring lesson of all underground movements: that power is never as total as it appears, and conscience is never as alone as it feels. From Munich classrooms to Afghan valleys, from Paris basements to Buenos Aires plazas, the record of human history shows that *where there is oppression, there will be imagination.* And where imagination survives, so too does the possibility of freedom.

War as a Cultural Sculptor:

War is often thought of as a destroyer—of lives, cities, governments, and social fabric. But what follows destruction is not always silence. Sometimes, it is *reinvention.* After the guns fall silent, a different kind of reckoning begins—less visible but no less vital. Art, literature, and music do not merely return after war; they re-emerge altered, charged with the weight of what has been lost, and with the urgency to make sense of what remains. These cultural expressions become diagnostic tools for nations in recovery—mirrors, maps, and megaphones for societies searching for identity in the rubble.

The aftermath of war forces a confrontation with fundamental questions: Who are we now? What should we remember? What must we forget? In this transitional space, culture becomes an arena of contested memory and redefined meaning. The Harlem Renaissance, while not directly a product of war in the conventional military sense, was profoundly shaped by the aftershocks of global and domestic violence—World War I, the 1919 Red Summer, and the systemic brutality of Jim Crow America. African American veterans returned from the trenches of Europe having fought for a democracy that denied them full citizenship at home. Their art became both protest and proclamation. Langston Hughes, Zora Neale Hurston, Aaron Douglas—these were not merely artists; they were architects of an alternative narrative, one that declared cultural autonomy in a nation that refused legal equality.

In this sense, post-war art often functions as both resistance and repair. Consider Dadaism, a movement born out of the grotesque absurdity of the First World War. Dada was not an aesthetic style; it was an *anti-style*, a deliberate revolt against the rationality and order that had justified mechanised slaughter. Artists like Hugo Ball and Hannah Höch turned to collage, absurdity, and nonsense as a way to expose the lie at the heart of modern civilisation: that logic and progress had inevitably led to trenches filled with rotting corpses. Dada was not escapism—it was confrontation by inversion. In rejecting coherence, it indicted a world that had become morally incoherent.

This cultural rupture can also be traced in Japanese post-war cinema. After the atomic bombings of Hiroshima and Nagasaki, Japanese filmmakers grappled with devastation on a scale previously unimaginable. But rather than dwell in spectacle, many directors pursued a more psychological excavation. Akira Kurosawa's *Ikiru* (1952) and *Rashomon* (1950) explore themes of mortality, justice, and the fragmentation of truth. These were not simply narratives about post-war recovery—they were meditations on moral ambiguity, on what it meant to live honestly in a society that had been profoundly complicit in violence. Meanwhile, films like Kaneto Shindō's *Children of Hiroshima* (1952) brought the trauma of the hibakusha—atomic bomb survivors—into the public eye, challenging state narratives that preferred rapid economic recovery to painful introspection.

This pattern repeats across geographies and generations. Post-genocide Rwanda, for instance, has seen a deliberate state-backed effort to use art and storytelling as a mode of reconciliation. The Rwandan government, through institutions like the National Unity and Reconciliation Commission, has supported theatre, poetry, and film projects designed to create space for shared mourning and future-building. These are not apolitical gestures. They are carefully structured attempts to rewrite the national story without erasing the rupture of 1994. The arts, in this context, are not merely expressive—they are instrumental in the shaping of *collective memory*.

Yet cultural reconstruction after war is not always state-directed. Sometimes it is subterranean, emerging not from policy but from pain. In the wake of the Vietnam War, American music experienced a reckoning. Folk, blues, and rock artists—Bob Dylan, Joan Baez, Marvin Gaye—translated national confusion and grief into melody. "What's Going On" was not just a hit; it was a requiem. The soundtrack of war's aftermath became a medium for democratic reflection. Similarly, the poetry of Wilfred Owen and Siegfried Sassoon during and after World War I did not glorify sacrifice—it exposed its grotesque futility. Their verses remain essential because they dared to speak what military communiqués never could: the brutal inner cost of following orders that defied human instinct.

What these varied examples share is a recognition that war deforms not only landscapes but *meanings*. And in the process of reassembly, culture assumes an almost diagnostic function. It becomes the site where trauma is transmuted—not erased—into something socially legible. One could argue that post-war culture is never merely a reflection of survival; it is an attempt to *ritualise* survival, to encode it into forms that can be shared, studied, and passed on.

But we should not romanticise this process. Cultural responses to war are not always noble or unifying. They can also be fractious, nostalgic, or regressive. The cultural mythologies that followed the American Civil War, particularly in the Southern United States, gave rise to the "Lost Cause" narrative—an elaborate cultural denial that romanticised the Confederacy and laid ideological groundwork for racial segregation. This underscores a critical point: *cultural sculpture after war is not inherently emancipatory; it can just as easily be a mechanism for revisionism*. The role of critical cultural literacy is to discern whether post-war creations are working toward truth or towards its obfuscation.

This tension is perhaps most visible in contemporary debates around public monuments, especially those tied to colonial or militaristic histories. What stories are being told in stone? Who is commemorated—and who is conspicuously absent? In cities like Bristol, Cape Town, and Richmond, statues have become flashpoints for broader discussions about historical memory and inherited trauma. These are not merely aesthetic debates—they are contests over the moral legacy of violence. *The post-war cultural sculptor is not always an artist; sometimes, it is a protestor with a rope.*

Even in literature, this sculpting function reveals the complexity of post-conflict identity. Consider the rise of magical realism in Latin America, emerging partly in the context of prolonged civil unrest and authoritarian regimes. Writers like Gabriel García Márquez and Isabel Allende used the surreal not as escapism but as a way to *truthfully capture what literal language could not.* Reality, fractured by war and repression, required a different grammar. The "magical" in their realism is less fantasy than a fidelity to emotional and historical complexity.

Crucially, post-war cultural production is not just reactive—it is generative. It seeds new ways of imagining society. Toni Morrison's *Beloved* is not just about the trauma of slavery; it's a meditation on how memory itself can be both redemptive and corrosive. Her novel reconstructs a world from shards, forcing readers to inhabit not just the historical facts of oppression, but the interiority of those who lived it. The cultural sculptor, then, is not merely assembling a monument—it is shaping a mirror, forcing a society to see itself whole, however painful that reflection may be.

Technological shifts have also changed the way post-war cultural sculpture manifests. Today, virtual reality, digital storytelling platforms, and AI-generated art are entering the field. Projects like *Clouds Over Sidra*, a VR film following a Syrian refugee girl, create an embodied empathy that traditional media struggles to evoke. As war becomes more asymmetric and dispersed, so too do its cultural responses. The challenge is to ensure these innovations deepen understanding rather than dilute it.

To understand war's aftermath is to understand that peace is not the end of conflict, but its mutation. Culture is how societies metabolise trauma, make sense of chaos, and reimagine what it means to be human after inhumanity. Whether through jazz riffs in Harlem, ink stains in Kigali, or frames of black-and-white film in Tokyo, post-war art asks: now that we know what we're capable of, what kind of world will we choose to make? That question is not answered in treaties or tribunals. It is answered in the stories we tell, the silences we break, and the futures we dare to imagine.

Chapter 5
Collapse and Rebirth

Victory parades, treaties inked in gilt-edged halls, triumphant headlines declaring "peace at last"—these are the familiar images that signal war's supposed conclusion. Yet, peel back the surface and the illusion falters. Peace, at least as conventionally understood, is a flimsy stand-in for genuine resolution. The guns may go silent, but their absence is quickly filled by other clamours: memory, grievance, vengeance, denial, ambition. The aftermath is no gentle return to the ordinary—it is an unsettled question mark. What follows the cessation of hostilities is rarely an end to history; more often, it is where history begins renegotiating its terms.

This is the fraught interval between collapse and whatever might follow—an interlude in which societies attempt, sometimes desperately, to translate catastrophe into meaning, or at least into a new order. Far from serving as an epilogue, the aftermath is a crucible where political identities, moral reckonings, and visions of the future are shaped and tested. In nations emerging from war, peace is never just the absence of artillery fire; it is a contested arena where old wounds, buried tensions, and rival aspirations jostle for supremacy. This struggle may take the form of tribunals and commissions. At other times, it re-emerges as uprisings dressed in the rhetoric of reform. Occasionally, it fosters genuine renewal—but almost never without extracting its price.

Consider the Treaty of Versailles. Meant to secure a lasting settlement after the First World War, it instead fertilised the soil for economic collapse, nationalist resurgence, and ultimately another global conflict. Its punitive measures revealed a profound misreading of what peace demands. Drafted and imposed without any real reconciliation among those who had borne the war's weight, Versailles became a textbook lesson in the futility of order built without justice, dignity, or psychological repair. On paper it may have resembled stability, but in practice it was a brittle construct destined to crack.

Such failures are not unique. Time and again, declarations of peace arrive prematurely, blithely overlooking the dense, interlocking ecosystems that must be rebuilt after conflict. The Cold War, for instance, never escalated into open combat between its main antagonists, yet its long shadow—proxy wars, espionage excesses, and political paranoia—showed that the absence of direct battle is hardly synonymous with healing. The missiles stayed in their silos, but the scaffolding of mistrust—surveillance states, ideological purges, nuclear brinkmanship—left a deeper imprint on global consciousness than many battlefields ever did. Peace, in that context, was not renewal but a frigid endurance.

So what does it mean to rebuild, whether a nation or a psyche, in war's wake? The German notion of *Vergangenheitsbewältigung*—literally, "coming to terms with the past"—offers one path. In the post-war decades, West Germany undertook an imperfect but significant reckoning: reformed curricula, public memorials, trials. Unlike Japan, where political sanitisation blunted acknowledgment of wartime guilt, Germany confronted its crimes with a degree of candour that astonished many. This was not merely the settling of accounts; it was an attempt to cultivate moral literacy. The Nuremberg Trials set a precedent: "following orders" could no longer shield atrocity, and the law itself could evolve in response to moral catastrophe.

Yet even here, the picture is uneven. Justice after conflict is never tidy. South Africa's Truth and Reconciliation Commission, under the guidance of Desmond Tutu, chose a markedly different route—favouring testimony and confession over punitive measures. Its legacy remains debated. Critics point to the lack of robust accountability; defenders argue it staved off a descent into civil war. What it revealed, however, is that transitional justice is as much theatre of the mind as it is of the law. It is concerned not only with punishing wrongdoers but with restoring legitimacy to the very concept of justice itself in places where it had long been absent.

Post-conflict landscapes often serve as laboratories for reimagining governance, morality, and even myth. Violence's end can yield not only grief but also a peculiar kind of creative momentum. Out of the wreckage of World War II emerged the United Nations and the

European Union—not naïve dreams, but deliberate experiments in preventing a repeat. Likewise, post-genocide Rwanda has pursued an ambitious, tightly controlled vision of national unity. Whether this amounts to genuine progress or to a rebranded authoritarianism remains contested, yet the scale of its civic reinvention cannot be denied.

On the human scale, the paradoxes are just as stark. For some survivors, peace is more destabilising than war. When daily life has been shaped by violence, its sudden absence can feel less like relief and more like vertigo. Veterans often speak of a disconnection from civilian existence—a sense that the "normal" world is the foreign one. This is more than post-traumatic stress; it is a dislocation of moral bearings. How does one relearn agency, when survival once required suspending moral choice altogether? In such moments, the work of reconstructing legal norms and national narratives is inseparable from the reintegration of individual conscience. Both are precarious. Both are indispensable.

It is also in the aftermath that stories of rebirth can conceal more troubling continuities. In the American telling of World War II, the "Greatest Generation" narrative frequently erases inconvenient truths: racial segregation in the armed forces, the internment of Japanese Americans, the limited recognition of women and minorities who sustained the war effort. The post-war boom did not lift all boats equally. Benefits like the G.I. Bill disproportionately advantaged white veterans. Renewal, therefore, is rarely shared without exclusion. One might ask: who gets to enjoy the harvest of peace, and who remains stranded in the ruins?

Yet, for all these shadows, the aftermath is also a space of radical possibility. It is here that dormant questions rise into the light: What shape should justice take when precedent is useless? How do we preserve the memory of atrocity without allowing it to fossilise into vengeance? Can grief be honoured without being weaponised? Some of the most compelling answers have come not from governments but from ordinary citizens. In Argentina, the Mothers of the Plaza de Mayo turned bereavement into political force. In Bosnia, youth-led digital storytelling seeks to bridge divides that formal agreements could not. These are acts of authorship by civilians, writing futures where official scripts have failed.

The argument, in essence, is that the aftermath is not the opposite of war—it is war's continuation in another register, its echo and residue, demanding interpretation. Peace, viewed through this lens, is not a point of arrival but a sustained discipline: the work of unearthing truths, tending to wounds, and crafting new social contracts. It is an active state, not a passive one. The true question is not whether societies can endure collapse, but whether they can transmute its legacy into something other than repetition.

In a century increasingly marked by drawn-out conflicts, climate upheaval, and mass displacement, the importance of understanding these post-war dynamics could hardly be greater. What we label "reconstruction" today will dictate the moral and political architecture of tomorrow. In that sense, this is not just a study of endings—it is a meditation on beginnings, and an invitation to reckon seriously with war's cost, not only in human lives but in the shaping of ideas. The labour of turning rupture into repair is arduous, but it remains the only work worth doing in the long shadow of catastrophe.

The Illusion of Peace:

Peace, it turns out, is often more performative than real. It arrives with signatures on parchment, public ceremonies, and the abrupt cessation of open violence—but not necessarily with justice, reconciliation, or security. The illusion of peace lies in its outward symbols: treaties, troop withdrawals, disarmament declarations. These imply finality, but what they frequently mask is a reconfiguration of conflict rather than its resolution. When we study the post-war settlements of the 20th century, particularly the Treaty of Versailles and the Cold War's diplomatic architecture, it becomes increasingly difficult to distinguish peace from deferred struggle. Both instances expose a deeper truth: that peace, as conventionally understood, is often not the end of war, but its mutation into another form.

The Treaty of Versailles, signed in June 1919, is one of modern history's most cited cases of peace turned provocation. Drafted by victors who saw negotiation as an opportunity for retribution, it imposed harsh economic reparations, territorial dismemberment, and a punitive war-guilt clause on a defeated Germany. On the surface, it was the formal cessation of World War I; in practice, it was a geopolitical pressure cooker. The treaty's most dangerous feature was not merely its content, but its *tone*—humiliating rather than restorative, calculated to subdue rather than reintegrate. This miscalculation wasn't just moral—it was strategic. By excluding Germany from the drafting process and denying it the dignity of participation, Versailles converted a military defeat into a civilisational grievance. It didn't bury the war; it buried a seed.

This seed would flourish in the interwar period through economic collapse, radicalisation, and the psychological aftershock of national emasculation. Far from stabilising Europe, Versailles destabilised it. The apparent peace of the 1920s was brittle, cosmetic. Beneath the veneer of diplomatic recovery lay the unacknowledged trauma of a system that had punished rather than rehabilitated. The result was the empowerment of extremism—not despite peace, but *because* of the kind of peace Versailles represented.

The deeper problem was epistemological: the assumption that peace is achieved by ending battle rather than repairing structure. Versailles, by refusing to reconstruct Europe's political and emotional scaffolding, created conditions under which another war was not only likely but almost inevitable. As historian Margaret MacMillan has argued, it was less a peace treaty than a temporary restraining order, enforced without consensus and designed without empathy. The illusion of peace, in this case, was not naivety—it was an act of willful neglect.

Contrast this with the Cold War, a period often mislabelled as an era of peace simply because direct conflict between superpowers was avoided. This binary—war versus non-war—obscures the fact that Cold War "peace" was deeply violent in both method and consequence. It featured dozens of proxy conflicts (Korea, Vietnam, Angola, Afghanistan), the proliferation of nuclear weapons, and the global entrenchment of authoritarian regimes under the guise of ideological loyalty. The language of peace was used liberally, but the architecture was built on fear, suspicion, and surveillance.

What distinguished the Cold War was its maintenance of stability through mutual threat. The doctrine of Mutually Assured Destruction (MAD) was not an expression of rational deterrence, as many political theorists optimistically argued, but a moral paradox. It hinged on the permanent readiness to destroy all life as the price for not doing so. In this context, "peace" was not the absence of violence, but the constant simulation of its possibility. States constructed entire foreign and domestic policies on the assumption that annihilation had to be *credible* in order to be avoided. This is not peace. It is institutionalised paranoia, disguised as stability.

Here, again, the illusion functions as a form of strategic theatre. Leaders spoke of dialogue and arms reduction while simultaneously increasing stockpiles and tightening internal controls. Intelligence agencies became the backbone of foreign policy, psychological operations blurred into diplomacy, and civil liberties were routinely compromised in the name of national security. For citizens on both sides of the ideological divide, the Cold War was not a reprieve from conflict, but its normalisation in subtler forms. It was, as Edward Said observed, a time when "culture became the battlefield."

Indeed, the Cold War's epistemology of peace shaped generations of thinkers, artists, and activists who began to question whether peace without justice could ever be legitimate. The civil rights movement in the United States, liberation struggles in the Global South, and dissident intellectuals in Eastern Europe were all, in a sense, responding to the cognitive dissonance of a world that claimed to be at peace while producing structural violence on a massive scale. Their critique was not simply political; it was conceptual. They challenged the idea that order, discipline, and containment constituted peace. Instead, they pointed to the quiet devastations—poverty, oppression, propaganda, racial violence—that proliferated in so-called peacetime.

What these case studies demonstrate is that peace is not an empirical condition to be observed; it is a *claim* to be interrogated. Who gets to declare peace? Who enforces it, who benefits from it, and who is excluded from its protections? These are not rhetorical questions. They define the contours of post-conflict politics. If we accept peace as merely the opposite of war, we cede enormous conceptual ground to those who can end shooting without addressing causality. We risk mistaking silence for consent, stillness for security.

The illusion of peace is particularly dangerous when it becomes self-justifying. Political elites invoke peace to suppress dissent, portray opposition as destabilising, or frame accountability efforts as reopening old wounds. This tendency was observable in post-Versailles Europe, where any critique of the treaty was labelled revisionist or unpatriotic, and again during the Cold War, when peace activists were routinely surveilled or smeared as traitors. The idea of peace, then, becomes a rhetorical weapon used to foreclose further debate—precisely when debate is most needed.

Moreover, peace as a static concept fails to account for the ways trauma lingers. Wars don't just kill bodies; they distort institutions, disfigure identities, and fragment narratives. The years following conflict are often characterised by a low-grade violence that lacks the drama of combat but not its consequences. These include economic hardship, forced migration, political instability, and unresolved psychological wounds. If peace is to mean anything more than the cessation of gunfire, it must grapple with these lived realities.

This requires a fundamental shift in our analytical lens. Rather than asking *when* peace begins, we must ask *how* it is constructed, maintained, and contested. This moves the discussion from treaties to processes, from silence to repair. It also invites humility: acknowledging that what appears as peace to one group may register as abandonment or even betrayal to another. The dissonance is not a flaw; it is a diagnostic. It reveals the unfinished work of justice, memory, and inclusion.

The concept of "positive peace," developed by Norwegian sociologist Johan Galtung, attempts to capture this shift. Unlike "negative peace"—the absence of violence—positive peace refers to the presence of conditions that sustain human flourishing: equity, participation, reconciliation, and truth. It demands more than demobilisation; it calls for rehumanisation. Galtung's insight challenges us to rethink the metrics by which we evaluate post-war outcomes. A peace that doesn't address structural inequalities or historical grievances is not peace—it is a delay mechanism.

Ultimately, the central argument of this subchapter is not that peace is unattainable, but that our definitions are insufficient. Treaties are necessary but not sufficient. Ceasefires matter, but they are only the beginning of a moral project. If we are serious about peace, we must stop thinking of it as a finish line and start treating it as a design challenge—a complex, adaptive system that requires maintenance, feedback, and reinvention. Only then can we move beyond illusions and begin the hard work of building something durable. Not merely the absence of war, but the presence of dignity.

Psychological Reconstruction:

There is a particular silence that follows war. It is not the stillness of recovery, but the vacuum left behind when a society confronts something too vast to articulate and too painful to deny. Physical reconstruction—buildings, roads, institutions—is measurable, visible, often politically incentivised. Psychological reconstruction, by contrast, is elusive, complex, and politically hazardous. Yet without it, the foundations of peace remain brittle. Post-conflict societies that fail to reckon with the psychic weight of collective trauma tend to carry forward unprocessed wounds, which later emerge as nationalism, denial, resentment, or even renewed violence. The question, then, is not simply how a nation rebuilds its infrastructure, but how it reconstructs its *conscience.*

Few countries have attempted this more systematically than post-war Germany. The term *Vergangenheitsbewältigung*, roughly translated as "coming to terms with the past", represents one of the most ambitious national projects of moral and psychological reckoning in modern history. Unlike many post-conflict settings where trauma is either buried under economic recovery or manipulated for political advantage, Germany's post-Holocaust evolution has centred on the premise that memory, if not confronted directly, will metastasise. The process was neither immediate nor uncontested. It took decades of generational turnover, legal trials, curricular reforms, and public debate for *Vergangenheitsbewältigung* to shift from a minority intellectual concern to a national ethos.

The early years after 1945 were marked more by amnesia than atonement. Denazification under Allied occupation was uneven and, in many cases, superficial. Many former Nazi officials were quietly reintegrated into post-war institutions under the rationale of bureaucratic continuity and Cold War expediency. For much of the 1950s, West Germany focused on economic rebirth—the so-called *Wirtschaftswunder* (economic miracle)—while psychological accountability lagged. It wasn't until the 1960s and 1970s, with the rise of a new post-war generation, that the moral architecture of *Vergangenheitsbewältigung* began to take shape. The children of perpetrators became the moral agitators, demanding transparency, remembrance, and justice.

One of the most significant catalysts was the Frankfurt Auschwitz Trials of 1963–1965. Unlike the earlier Nuremberg Trials, which were largely imposed by external powers, the Frankfurt proceedings were conducted by Germans, against Germans, for crimes committed on German soil. Their cultural impact went far beyond jurisprudence. They shattered the myth that the Holocaust was the work of a few madmen and exposed the bureaucratic banality of genocide—the way ordinary individuals, not just fanatics, enabled systemic evil. This realisation reframed the moral landscape of post-war Germany: complicity was no longer deniable, and innocence was no longer assumed.

Education became a frontline in the psychological reconstruction process. German school curricula were rewritten to include detailed accounts of Nazi atrocities. Memorials and museums proliferated—not just to honour victims, but to confront the national conscience. Public commemoration was deliberately uncomfortable. The Holocaust Memorial in Berlin, for instance, is not a place of serenity; its disorienting concrete slabs are meant to unsettle. The message is clear: remembrance is not about closure; it is about vigilance.

What makes Germany's model particularly instructive is that it does not frame trauma as a rupture to be forgotten, but as a civic responsibility to be carried. Memory becomes a discipline—an act of sustained engagement rather than a static monument. This approach challenges conventional post-conflict narratives that equate healing with forgetting. In contrast, *Vergangenheitsbewältigung* insists that the psychological health of a nation depends on its capacity to hold discomfort without collapsing into denial or deflection.

This has powerful implications for other societies navigating their own legacies of violence. In post-apartheid South Africa, for example, the Truth and Reconciliation Commission (TRC) was an attempt to reckon with systemic injustice not by erasing history, but by surfacing it. Victims gave testimony, perpetrators were offered conditional amnesty, and the process was televised—a deliberate strategy to make private pain a matter of public consciousness. Yet the South African experience also reveals the limits of psychological reconstruction without material transformation. While the TRC helped frame a new national narrative, it could not on its own dismantle the structural inequalities inherited from apartheid. The result has been a fragile peace, increasingly strained by unmet expectations.

In Rwanda, following the 1994 genocide, psychological reconstruction took yet another form: community-based *gacaca* courts, where survivors and perpetrators confronted one another in open-air hearings. These were not trials in the Western legal sense but rituals of disclosure, apology, and forgiveness. The goal was not simply to punish, but to reweave the social fabric. At their best, *gacaca* courts allowed for local ownership of justice and catalysed emotional closure; at their worst, they risked retraumatising victims or enabling false reconciliation. Still, they reflect a vital insight: psychological healing after mass violence often depends not on institutions alone, but on culture—on the stories people tell, the rituals they enact, and the moral language available to them.

Each of these examples underscores a broader point: trauma is not just personal, it is political. And recovery is not just therapeutic, it is ethical. The work of psychological reconstruction demands both introspection and institutional reform. It must acknowledge not only what was done, but *why* it was allowed to happen—and how future societies can build resilience against repetition. This means investing in education that cultivates historical literacy and ethical imagination.

It means supporting arts and literature that give voice to suppressed narratives. And it means creating legal and civic structures that encourage truth-telling without collapsing into vengeance.

One of the most difficult aspects of psychological reconstruction is its temporal nature. It does not follow a predictable arc. It can take decades—or longer—for societies to admit the depth of their wounds, let alone treat them. This is especially true when trauma has been normalised. In the United States, for instance, the legacy of slavery, segregation, and racial violence has never been fully metabolised. Efforts at reckoning—whether through educational reform, reparations debate, or public memorials—remain contested and incomplete. Yet the German case demonstrates that transformation is possible, even if belated. It is not inevitability that shapes a nation's moral trajectory, but *will*.

Importantly, psychological reconstruction is not the opposite of accountability; it is its companion. Without justice, memory can be performative. Without memory, justice can be vindictive. The most effective post-conflict societies recognise that healing requires both legal clarity and emotional complexity. They avoid the trap of choosing between remembering and moving on. Instead, they institutionalise remembrance *as* movement—forward-looking, but not forgetful.

There is also a generational dimension that must be acknowledged. Psychological reconstruction often begins in earnest only when those closest to the violence are no longer in power. The second and third generations are usually the ones who interrogate the myths their parents lived by. This temporal lag is not a failure; it is an anthropological reality. Collective trauma often produces a protective silence, which only begins to lift when new voices demand to be heard. The task of reconstruction, then, is not just to support those who remember, but to prepare those who will inherit the memory.

Ultimately, what distinguishes psychological reconstruction from other forms of post-war recovery is that it refuses the lure of false catharsis. It does not seek to close the book, but to reread it with clearer eyes. It is slow, messy, and often uncomfortable. But it is also the most profound investment a society can make in its own humanity. Because when nations learn to confront their darkest chapters—not as aberrations, but as instructive failures—they develop the moral reflexes necessary to avoid repetition. Peace, in this sense, is not just negotiated; it is *cultivated*, in the deep and often painful soil of historical truth.

Transitional Justice and the Fragility of Truth:

Transitional justice occupies one of the most treacherous spaces in post-conflict reconstruction. It attempts the impossible: to turn memory into evidence, trauma into testimony, and politics into morality. It must satisfy competing imperatives—truth and reconciliation, punishment and peace, individual accountability and collective healing. Most critically, it must do this in societies that are neither stable nor unified, where institutions are fragile and the past is not yet past. Transitional justice does not begin with clarity or consensus. It begins with brokenness—and the urgent question of what kind of future can be built upon it.

The Nuremberg Trials in the aftermath of the Second World War are often treated as the gold standard of post-conflict justice. They were, in many respects, a legal watershed: the first international prosecution of crimes against humanity, the rejection of "just following orders" as a defence, and the articulation of new moral categories that placed universal human rights above sovereign impunity. But even Nuremberg, the most carefully staged of tribunals, was riddled with tensions. The trials were conducted by victors, not neutrals. They excluded scrutiny of Allied actions such as the Dresden bombings or the Soviet atrocities in Katyn. Justice, it seemed, had boundaries shaped not just by law, but by power.

Yet Nuremberg's significance lies precisely in this tension. It marked a pivotal moment when the international community acknowledged that war crimes were not just military offences, but affronts to civilisation itself. It created a vocabulary—genocide, crimes against humanity, aggression—that would shape future tribunals and human rights discourse. But it also illustrated the fragility of truth in a post-war context. When justice is administered by those with vested interests, the line between moral reckoning and political theatre is dangerously thin.

South Africa's Truth and Reconciliation Commission (TRC), established after the end of apartheid in 1994, took a radically different approach. Instead of punitive trials, it offered amnesty in exchange for full disclosure. Victims were invited to speak publicly about their suffering. Perpetrators who confessed truthfully could avoid prosecution. The TRC's design was rooted in pragmatism: a full judicial reckoning was logistically impossible, and the priority was peaceful transition, not retribution. But it also reflected a deeper philosophical shift: that truth-telling could itself be a form of justice.

The TRC's strength was its visibility. It turned justice into national theatre, allowing a fractured society to bear witness to itself. Its weakness was its conditionality. Many victims never saw their abusers brought to trial. Some perpetrators offered evasive or partial confessions. And the structural legacies of apartheid—economic inequality, spatial segregation, and institutional distrust—remained largely intact. As Archbishop Desmond Tutu, who chaired the Commission, later acknowledged, truth without transformation risks becoming performative. *Reconciliation*, he wrote, *is not cheap. It must be accompanied by reparation, restitution, and systemic change.*

The question of justice after mass violence is not only about what to punish, but *how* to narrate. In the civil wars of Sierra Leone (1991–2002), where atrocities included child soldiering, mass amputations, and sexual violence, the UN-backed Special Court faced enormous constraints: limited resources, political interference, and a traumatised population. Yet it managed to establish important precedents, including the first conviction of individuals for using child soldiers and for conflict-related sexual slavery. The Court also made a deliberate choice to prosecute not just rebels but also government-aligned forces—an attempt to demonstrate neutrality and restore public trust.

But legal success does not always translate into societal healing. Many Sierra Leoneans viewed the Court as remote and elitist, disconnected from the local realities of reconciliation. Traditional justice mechanisms, such as community-based "fambul tok" (family talk), often did more to restore trust than the distant proclamations of judges in robes. This highlights a recurring dilemma: formal justice may offer international legitimacy, but it rarely satisfies the cultural or emotional needs of traumatised communities.

The post-war landscape in Bosnia-Herzegovina illustrates an even starker problem: when transitional justice occurs in a context where truth itself is politicised beyond repair. The International Criminal Tribunal for the former Yugoslavia (ICTY), established in 1993, documented extensive evidence of war crimes, including the Srebrenica genocide and the siege of Sarajevo. It indicted high-level figures across all ethnic factions, and its rulings contributed significantly to international criminal jurisprudence. Yet in Bosnia today, denialism is rampant. War criminals are venerated as heroes in some communities. School textbooks tell divergent histories. Ethno-nationalist parties continue to exploit divisions rather than bridge them.

The ICTY, while legally rigorous, failed to generate a shared moral consensus. It created *facts* but not *truth*—because truth in post-conflict societies is not simply an aggregation of evidence; it is a contested narrative, shaped by identity, memory, and fear. The very notion of "transitional justice" assumes a transition—from conflict to peace, from fragmentation to cohesion. But when that transition stalls, justice becomes a ghost: visible in international archives, but absent in daily life.

These case studies expose the paradox at the heart of transitional justice: *truth is essential, but inherently fragile.* It must be constructed amid ruins, negotiated among enemies, and sustained through institutions that are often themselves complicit in past abuses. There is no neutral ground. Every decision—who is tried, who is pardoned, what stories are told—reverberates politically.

Moreover, transitional justice raises uncomfortable questions about the relationship between justice and peace. Can they always coexist? Or must one be sacrificed for the other? The Nuremberg model pursued legal clarity, but it was made possible by total military victory. The South African model favoured peace over retribution, but left many victims feeling unfulfilled. The Bosnian model prioritised international norms, but failed to integrate them into the national psyche. There is no perfect balance—only trade-offs.

One recurring insight across contexts is that justice must be *seen* to be done. Transparency, accessibility, and public participation are not luxuries; they are essential components of legitimacy. This does not mean justice must always be forgiving. In some cases, impunity corrodes social trust far more than harsh sentencing would. But the process must be intelligible and participatory. Closed-door settlements, elite bargains, or technocratic interventions may stabilise regimes, but they rarely heal societies.

Another insight is that *timing* matters. Immediate post-conflict periods are often ill-suited to comprehensive justice. Emotions run high, institutions are weak, and political alliances are volatile. In such moments, calls for accountability may be drowned out by demands for stability. Yet delay can also breed cynicism. The longer justice is deferred, the more it risks being perceived as arbitrary, irrelevant, or vindictive. Transitional justice, then, is not just a legal task but a *political choreography*—a sequencing of trials, testimonies, reforms, and memorials that together shape a society's moral direction.

In the digital age, transitional justice faces new challenges. Social media can amplify victim testimonies, but also disinformation. Surveillance technologies can gather forensic evidence, but also infringe on privacy. AI tools can analyse war crimes documentation, but also be weaponised by authoritarian regimes. As transitional justice enters this era, it must grapple with the dual imperative of technological capability and ethical restraint. The fragility of truth today is not just a political problem; it is a *technological* one as well.

At its core, transitional justice is a bet: that societies can emerge from atrocity not only intact, but wiser. That human dignity, once violated, can be reaffirmed through reasoned process. But it is also a fragile undertaking—dependent on memory, political will, institutional design, and the unpredictability of human response. It is not a single act, but a generational effort. And it must be constantly re-earned.

This subchapter is not an argument for one model over another. It is an invitation to think rigorously about the conditions under which truth can survive political rupture. To ask not just what justice looks like, but what it *feels* like for those who must live with its outcomes. And to recognise that the aftermath of conflict is not a blank slate, but a volatile terrain where the struggle for meaning continues long after the shooting stops. The work of transitional justice, if taken seriously, does not resolve this struggle—it dignifies it.

The Resilient Imagination:

One of the least examined yet most profound consequences of war is what happens when the guns fall silent—not merely in terms of rebuilding what was lost, but reimagining what is possible. Amidst the physical devastation, social fracture, and moral exhaustion of post-conflict societies, a peculiar kind of cognitive energy emerges. It is not born of triumph, but of necessity. Where institutions collapse and ideological certainties disintegrate, space opens for the *resilient imagination*—a force that does not just restore the past but rewrites the future.

War, by its very nature, deconstructs. It dismantles borders, belief systems, hierarchies, and the bureaucratic inertia of the pre-war order. But this destruction—however catastrophic—also disrupts calcified assumptions and inherited orthodoxies. The post-conflict moment, for all its human cost, often becomes an accidental clearing. And into that void, thinkers, dreamers, and reformers step—not always welcomed, but rarely absent. *What if*, they ask, *we did not rebuild what was, but invented what could be?*

This dynamic was visible in post-World War II Japan, where defeat and occupation forced the nation to confront not only physical ruin but spiritual implosion. The Meiji-era imperial mythos had crumbled. Hiroshima and Nagasaki had rendered any return to nationalist militarism morally impossible and strategically obsolete. But instead of clinging to nostalgia or seeking vengeance, Japan's post-war architects embraced reinvention. The 1947 constitution, drafted under Allied supervision but shaped by Japanese intellectuals, enshrined pacifism in Article 9—a clause that remains fiercely debated to this day. More broadly, Japan became a laboratory for economic transformation, urban design, and cultural introspection. Post-war cinema—especially in the hands of directors like Akira Kurosawa and Yasujirō Ozu—articulated a quiet reckoning: the characters they portrayed were not heroes, but humans emerging from rubble, searching for coherence in a world stripped of ideology.

In the aftermath of the Rwandan genocide, the government of national unity did not simply aim to prevent further violence; it attempted to reimagine what it meant to be Rwandan. The old categories—Hutu and Tutsi—were officially abolished. National identity was no longer ethnic, but civic. This was not merely political expedience. It was a strategic act of narrative engineering. Schools, media, and public ceremonies were mobilised to construct a post-genocidal mythos: one rooted in reconciliation, resilience, and shared purpose. Critics have rightly noted that this top-down reimagining carries risks, including authoritarian overreach and suppression of dissent. Yet it remains one of the clearest examples of how the resilient imagination can operate not only in literature or philosophy but in *statecraft.*

Post-war societies often give rise to unexpected philosophical experiments because they operate outside the conventional pressures of status quo politics. In the wake of war, there is no status quo to protect. Consider post-World War I Europe, where the shell-shocked intelligentsia rejected the rationalism and nationalism that had driven the continent into the abyss. The Dada movement, born in neutral Zurich among displaced artists and thinkers, expressed its anti-war politics not through manifestos but through absurdism, satire, and visual chaos. Dada was not a call for reform—it was a rejection of meaning itself. And yet, in doing so, it opened the door to new forms of artistic rebellion, many of which would shape modernism for decades.

One cannot overlook the role of myth-making in these periods. Post-war societies do not simply record what happened; they construct narratives about what it *meant.* These narratives are not always accurate, nor are they purely manipulative. They serve a necessary psychological and cultural function. In post-Civil War United States, both the North and South developed distinct mythologies. The North institutionalised a vision of Union and emancipation, while the South romanticised the "Lost Cause"—a narrative that would later entrench Jim Crow. These mythologies were not products of war alone, but of what war left behind: unresolved grief, political contestation, and the hunger for coherent identity.

In Eastern Europe, the collapse of Soviet hegemony in the 1990s triggered not just geopolitical reordering, but a collective rethinking of values, aesthetics, and public life. Cities like Berlin became hubs of cultural experimentation, where formerly marginalised voices—queer communities, immigrant artists, underground intellectuals—began shaping the social imagination. The physical scars of war and occupation were not erased but integrated into public architecture and discourse. The past was not hidden; it was displayed, critiqued, repurposed.

What these cases reveal is that post-conflict periods are not blank slates, but *contested fields*. The resilient imagination does not unfold uncontested. Authoritarian regimes often use trauma to justify control, invoking stability as a pretext for suppression. Extremist groups may exploit collective suffering to advance revanchist agendas. The imaginative potential of a post-war moment is fragile, because the very freedom it offers is volatile. This is why the role of civil society, education, media, and art becomes so central. These are the arenas in which the contours of the post-war imagination are debated, rehearsed, and realised.

The civic reinvention that often follows war is not simply a moral luxury; it is a political necessity. After the Yugoslav wars, grassroots organisations in Bosnia and Serbia worked not only on humanitarian relief but on crafting new spaces for dialogue and youth engagement. Theatre groups staged plays that explored interethnic trauma. Independent radio stations aired stories from both sides of the conflict. These efforts were small in scale but immense in significance. They seeded a pluralistic sensibility that legal mechanisms and peace treaties alone could not create.

At its most ambitious, the resilient imagination manifests in constitutional design. The post-apartheid South African constitution was not a mere compromise between warring factions; it was a moral and aspirational document that embedded equality, dignity, and human rights into the DNA of the new state. It went beyond conflict resolution and ventured into the terrain of ethical vision. Similarly, the post-genocide Cambodian constitution attempted—however imperfectly—to reconcile traditional monarchy with modern democratic norms. These were not merely technical instruments. They were expressions of a collective gamble: that people brutalised by war could still imagine—and institutionalise—dignity.

Utopian thinking, often dismissed as naïve, plays a crucial role in these contexts. It provides the imaginative scaffolding necessary to move from survival to meaning. When a society has seen the worst of itself, imagining the best is not fantasy—it is resistance. Of course, not all utopian projects succeed. Some are co-opted. Others descend into new forms of orthodoxy. But their existence matters because they stretch the horizon of what is considered thinkable.

This resilience of imagination also operates on an individual level. Post-traumatic growth is a documented psychological phenomenon in which survivors of severe trauma report newfound clarity of purpose, redefined values, and deeper interpersonal connections. While it is not universal, and should never be romanticised, it suggests that collapse does not preclude growth. The same is true of communities. Collective trauma, while devastating, can incubate a different kind of awareness—of what was taken for granted, what must be protected, and what ought to be reimagined.

Technology, too, now plays a role in shaping the resilient imagination. In Syria, despite ongoing war, digital artists and activists have created immersive archives, AI-powered documentation tools, and virtual memorials that preserve cultural memory under siege. In Ukraine, artists and architects have already begun sketching out post-conflict reconstruction plans, integrating ecological sustainability and participatory design into their blueprints. These are not just speculative exercises; they are acts of defiance against despair.

It is tempting to see post-war imagination as a luxury—something that happens after the real work of justice, reconstruction, and diplomacy is done. But history suggests otherwise. The societies that recover most meaningfully are not always those that rebuild fastest or prosecute most thoroughly. They are those that make space for difficult conversations, honour complexity, and dare to imagine futures that are not merely *less violent*, but more just, more inclusive, and more humane.

The resilient imagination, then, is not a romantic abstraction. It is a strategic resource. It allows post-conflict societies to redefine legitimacy, rebuild trust, and reclaim moral agency. It operates through symbols, laws, stories, rituals, and institutions. And it begins not when peace is declared, but when people look at the devastation and ask—not how to go back, but how to go forward differently.

This subchapter has traced the myriad ways in which imagination survives war, and how, against all odds, it becomes a tool not just for recovery, but for reinvention. In doing so, it affirms a simple but vital truth: while war may rupture the body of a society, the imagination—when nurtured—can heal its mind.

Chapter 6
When Children Lead Armies

Children do not choose war. Yet history, with unsettling regularity, shows war choosing them—drafting them into its machinery, bending their loyalties, and leaving marks that time alone cannot erase. Our usual image of conflict is an adult affair: uniforms, command structures, grand causes. But the inclusion of children—whether they march with rifles, sit in classrooms warped by ideology, serve as symbols, or endure as survivors—signals a deeper rupture, one that slices through not only the battlefield but the very fabric of civilisation. To ask what happens when children lead armies is not a clever paradox. It is to stare into the most grotesque inversion of innocence, and perhaps the most urgent moral dilemma of our age.

This is not a marginal tragedy; it is a structural reality. From Sierra Leone's drugged and armed boy soldiers to the ranks of Hitler Youth, from the "caliphate cubs" of ISIS to any number of indoctrinated youth brigades, children have been repeatedly deployed as weapons, messengers, and symbols. Their bodies become implements; their minds, contested terrain. Yet this grim truth offers not only cause for grief, but a lens—showing how identity is forged under coercion, how memory shatters under prolonged trauma, and how healing must be reimagined when the wound is inflicted before adulthood even begins.

The very phrase "child soldier" feels like it should collapse under its own contradiction. And still, through the 20th and 21st centuries, from Liberia and Uganda to Myanmar and Colombia, children as young as eight have been abducted, coerced, or persuaded into militias. Some take up weapons; others haul supplies, spy on villages, or serve as living shields. What binds them is not their function, but their perceived disposability by those who command them. The youth of a recruit becomes a calculated advantage: pliable minds, swift obedience, and scant moral resistance to orders scarcely comprehended. When the guns fall silent, their war is not over. They emerge needing far more than schooling—they require the painstaking work of rebuilding identity, restoring trust, and returning to communities that may see them not as victims, but as culpable.

These truths force us to reconsider what we mean by "childhood." If childhood rests on play, trust, and a gradual initiation into society, then war deliberately demolishes each foundation. Yet it also reshapes the definition. In Stalin's Soviet Union, education was not about curiosity but about loyalty—training young eyes to watch, ears to overhear, tongues to report. Hitler Youth followed the same logic: the child was a raw material, to be moulded before rival visions of the world could take root. Modern groups such as Boko Haram or ISIS refine these tactics with chilling precision. They cut children off from families, wall them in from competing stories, and craft identity through terror, ritual, and repetition. This is not education gone wrong; it is education weaponised.

To grasp this manipulation, one must move beyond policy briefings and into the terrain of psychology. Children process trauma differently from adults. They often lack the vocabulary for what they have endured; instead, trauma leaks through behaviour—withdrawal, sudden violence, recurrent nightmares, or eerie silence. Aid workers in displacement camps report drawings that feature not homes or dreams, but corpses and guns. Play becomes an act of re-enactment; art becomes a record. Such expressions defy therapeutic approaches rooted in conversation. For these children, recovery often begins with recognition—that their trauma resides as much in the body and imagination as in memory.

And still, there are moments of reclamation. Across post-conflict landscapes—from Africa to Asia to the Middle East—NGOs, educators, and artists have worked alongside young survivors to transform memory into meaning. In northern Uganda, UNICEF programmes paired former child soldiers with village elders, creating spaces for ritualised dialogue rather than courtroom confession. In Colombia, demobilised youths have taken to the stage, narrating their histories in theatre rather than in formal testimony. These acts do not undo the past. But they challenge the narrative, offering young people a shift from objects of pity or suspicion to authors of their own story. That is not mere rehabilitation—it is a reclamation of agency.

Such work forces us to revisit the question of justice. International law, even with provisions such as the Rome Statute's ban on recruiting fighters under fifteen, struggles to decide: is a child soldier a victim, a perpetrator, or both? The answers are uneven, and so is enforcement. In many post-war communities, returned child combatants face hostility from neighbours who suffered at their hands. In others, silence is encouraged—stories left untold to avoid reopening wounds. In these circumstances, storytelling is not simply cathartic; it becomes a form of moral repair. Speaking returns authorship to the child; listening returns conscience to the community.

Yet the damage is not only physical or legal. War manipulates the very architecture of the imagination. The myths, stories, and roles assigned to children shape how they understand loyalty, justice, and identity long after the fighting stops. A child raised on tales of glorious martyrdom may grow into an adult who believes violence redeems. One trained to see "the other" as less than human may never fully join a pluralistic society. Thus, peacebuilding cannot stop at disarmament or reconstruction. It must address narrative repair—changing not only what children believe, but the way they learn to believe.

This, then, is not just an account of youth caught in conflict. It is an inquiry into how war can redefine youth itself—how states and armed movements conspire in the weaponisation of innocence, and how societies must respond with educational, therapeutic, and cultural strategies that see children not merely as casualties to be rescued, but as citizens to be empowered.

Confronting this reality means shedding illusions. War is not always imposed on children from without; sometimes it is channelled through them. Propaganda targeting the young is not a relic of the 20th century but a living tactic. And a sentimental ideal of childhood, however comforting, can obscure the scale and precision of its exploitation.

Ultimately, the line between victim and participant blurs when the young are drawn into war's orbit. Trauma takes root before it can be spoken. And the restoration of youth is inseparable from the restoration of a shared future. How children are treated in wartime is not a footnote to history—it is one of its central moral tests. To truly understand war, we must reckon with what it does to those too young to speak its language, yet old enough to bear its weight. That may be the most crucial story of all.

The Lost Generations:

The phrase "child soldier" should not exist. It collapses two incompatible ideas—innocence and violence—into one brutal reality. And yet across modern history, in countries such as Liberia, Uganda, Myanmar, the Democratic Republic of Congo, Colombia, and beyond, children have been conscripted, abducted, indoctrinated, and transformed into instruments of warfare. They are the foot soldiers of fractured states and failed peace processes. Their weapons are not just rifles, but broken trust, manipulated identities, and stolen childhoods. This is not merely a human rights issue; it is a profound crisis of political imagination and ethical responsibility. The psychological and cultural consequences extend far beyond the battlefield. They deform entire generations.

Children are not simply "young adults" in war—they are uniquely vulnerable and uniquely valuable. Their malleability, loyalty, and lack of developed moral agency make them desirable recruits for militias and armed factions. In the civil wars of Liberia and Sierra Leone during the 1990s and early 2000s, child soldiers were not incidental. They were central. Charles Taylor's forces, like the Revolutionary United Front in Sierra Leone, deliberately used children for reconnaissance, terror operations, and front-line combat. Some were given drugs to desensitise them. Others were forced to kill family members to sever emotional ties and ensure loyalty through complicity. The systematic use of children was not a breakdown of order. It *was* the order.

The logic of such conscription is chilling in its pragmatism. Children are easier to intimidate, less likely to defect, and more willing to follow arbitrary commands. A study conducted by the Coalition to Stop the Use of Child Soldiers noted that underage recruits often internalised violent roles more thoroughly than adults, precisely because they lacked competing identities to anchor them. In other words, the soldier role didn't replace the child—it *became* the child. And this fusion of identity and violence is what makes the psychological aftermath so enduring.

The post-conflict phase is often mistakenly framed as a return to normalcy. But for former child soldiers, normal is a concept without reference. Many return to communities that fear them, stigmatise them, or blame them for atrocities. Reintegration is not merely logistical—it is existential. Who is a child that has killed? Who is a child that has commanded others to die? These are not questions for courtrooms alone; they are questions for culture, education, religion, and social memory. In northern Uganda, where the Lord's Resistance Army abducted over 30,000 children over two decades, former combatants face rejection not just from peers but from their own families. In some cases, traditional cleansing rituals have been reintroduced to symbolically "wash away" the violence. These rituals are not anachronisms—they are functional psychological technologies, standing in for absent state infrastructure.

The cultural damage, however, is not limited to the individual. Entire societies are altered when their youth are militarised. The myths that sustain a society—about protection, development, future—become hollow. The figure of the child, once a symbol of continuity, becomes a symbol of collapse. In Myanmar, both the military junta and rebel groups like the Kachin Independence Army have relied on child fighters. The normalisation of child soldiers in some regions has led to a generational erosion of trust: if a boy with a gun can be your neighbour's son, who is safe? Who is innocent? The result is a creeping fatalism, where violence becomes not just a tool but a habit of being.

And then there is the internal landscape—the psychological fallout that often goes unspoken. Former child soldiers experience high rates of PTSD, dissociation, depression, and aggression. But their symptoms often defy standard clinical models. Their trauma is cumulative, not episodic. It is not one event but the slow, daily corrosion of empathy and safety. Many do not remember a time before war. Others misremember it. Healing in such contexts cannot simply rely on psychiatric intervention—it must involve storytelling, ritual, art, community, and alternative models of justice. In Liberia, the Truth and Reconciliation Commission took statements from both perpetrators and victims—many of whom were one and the same. The act of speaking, in this context, was not just testimonial. It was reconstructive.

It is important to note that not all former child soldiers are traumatised in the same way. Some find resilience in faith, mentorship, or restructured schooling. Others draw on cultural or familial anchors that survived the war. The problem lies in systems, not individuals. Most post-war recovery programmes are underfunded, short-term, and politically fragile. Reintegration efforts often treat youth as broken objects to be repaired, rather than agents to be equipped. The consequence is a revolving door of exclusion: many rejoin armed groups not because they are violent, but because they are invisible.

There is also a difficult philosophical question that looms over the topic: to what extent are child soldiers culpable for what they did? The law offers limited guidance. The Rome Statute prohibits the recruitment of children under 15, but says little about how to handle underage perpetrators. In the Special Court for Sierra Leone, some children were used as witnesses, while others were quietly sidelined. Public trials of child soldiers are rare, not just for legal reasons but for moral ones. There is deep discomfort in holding a 14-year-old accountable for a massacre—especially when that child was coerced, indoctrinated, or drugged. But avoiding the question entirely leaves victims without recognition and perpetrators without reckoning. Justice must be contextual, not merely legalistic.

Part of the solution lies in education—not just for the children, but for the societies to which they return. In Rwanda, post-genocide schools incorporated history lessons that attempted to name what happened, assign responsibility, and imagine a shared future. In Uganda, some NGOs used storytelling workshops where former child soldiers wrote fictionalised versions of their lives—not to obscure facts, but to create emotional distance from them. These stories were sometimes published or performed, offering not only catharsis but narrative legitimacy. They allowed the child to be a subject, not merely a case.

The international community also bears responsibility. The recruitment of child soldiers is not an isolated atrocity; it is a predictable feature of under-governed or conflict-ridden states. And yet foreign aid is often reactive rather than anticipatory. Funding flows in during crisis and dries up during peace. But the deepest work—rebuilding trust, rewriting identity, restoring agency—happens in the quiet years after the guns have gone silent. It is then that societies must decide whether to treat former child soldiers as liabilities or as future leaders. And that decision shapes everything.

The term "lost generation" is often invoked to describe youth destroyed by war. But this phrasing can be dangerously reductive. These children are not lost. They were taken. They were manipulated, brutalised, and then often discarded. But loss is not destiny. The more appropriate term may be *interrupted generation*—one whose development was hijacked but not foreclosed. Recovery, when it occurs, is not a return but a re-invention. It requires more than sympathy; it requires structural imagination.

This article, then, is not a catalogue of suffering. It is a call to seriousness. To examine child soldiers is not merely to condemn war—it is to understand its mechanisms, to see how deeply violence can embed itself in the making of a person. It is to confront the moral costs of policies and the psychological residue of conflict. And most importantly, it is to ask what kind of adulthood is possible when childhood has been conscripted. The answer is not simple. But the question cannot be avoided.

"Propaganda and the Shaping of Young Minds":

The manipulation of children during wartime is not a tactical error. It is often a deliberate act of ideological engineering. Totalitarian regimes and militant movements alike have long recognised that if you wish to ensure obedience tomorrow, you must begin by reconfiguring identity today. The shaping of young minds in conflict is not merely a footnote in political history—it is one of the clearest demonstrations of how power thinks long-term. And while bullets may win battles, it is ideas—planted early and relentlessly—that shape the battlefield of belief.

The modern prototype of state-sponsored youth indoctrination was perhaps most systematised under Nazi Germany. The Hitlerjugend (Hitler Youth), established in the 1920s and made compulsory by 1936, was not simply a youth organisation—it was a nation-building apparatus. Boys were trained not only in physical drills and pseudo-military tactics but in racial ideology, loyalty to Führer and Fatherland, and the virtues of sacrifice. Girls in the Bund Deutscher Mädel (League of German Girls) were inculcated with the centrality of motherhood to the Reich and the racial purity of German bloodlines. This was not education—it was identity fabrication. By bypassing the family and embedding ideology directly into school curricula, youth organisations, literature, and even toys, the Nazi regime effectively drafted children into its war of ideas years before it mobilised them for war of arms.

Soviet indoctrination under Stalin followed a similar trajectory, though wrapped in different moral justifications. The Komsomol, the youth wing of the Communist Party, positioned young people as heroic vanguards of the proletariat. Education was rigidly controlled, history was rewritten in favour of Marxist-Leninist narratives, and religion was methodically dismantled. Children were encouraged to report dissident behaviour—including that of their parents. Loyalty to the state was not just a virtue; it was a higher allegiance than loyalty to family. The case of Pavlik Morozov, a boy celebrated for denouncing his father as a "kulak" enemy of the state, became a national parable. Whether factually accurate or fabricated, the story's value lay in what it demanded of young citizens: to displace moral ambiguity with ideological clarity. And in doing so, it redefined virtue as obedience, and betrayal as heroism.

What unites these regimes is not just their authoritarianism, but their sophisticated grasp of narrative psychology. They understood that children are not simply empty vessels waiting to be filled—they are active meaning-makers. And the earlier one intercepts the meaning-making process, the more profound the impact. That is why totalitarian systems target mythologies, symbols, and rituals. They recast ancient traditions, hijack cultural artefacts, and replace complexity with certainties. Propaganda aimed at children is rarely subtle, because it doesn't need to be. What it needs is repetition, consistency, and emotional hooks.

The Islamic State (ISIS) offers a chilling 21st-century iteration of this dynamic. In the territories it controlled in Syria and Iraq, ISIS established schooling systems that fused religious indoctrination with militaristic training. Children were not merely taught Islamic doctrine—they were taught a perverted version engineered to justify violence, martyrdom, and sectarian hatred. "Cubs of the Caliphate" videos featured children executing prisoners, planting bombs, and pledging loyalty to the caliph. These were not accidental propaganda tools—they were deliberate spectacles, designed to recruit, terrify, and signal the next generation of jihad. In ISIS's logic, youth was not a developmental stage—it was an opportunity to lock identity into an unbreakable mould before pluralism or empathy could take hold.

What makes this kind of manipulation so psychologically potent is that it often masquerades as empowerment. Children are told they are not too young to matter. They are warriors, agents of history, moral actors in a corrupted world. That offer—of significance, belonging, and purpose—is a powerful psychological lure, especially in societies fractured by conflict, inequality, or humiliation. Whether in interwar Germany, Stalinist Russia, or the Syrian civil war, the story told to children is always the same: the world is broken, but you can help fix it—if you believe, obey, and fight.

The long-term damage of such indoctrination is not merely cognitive—it is emotional and moral. Children who are taught to demonise outsiders, glorify violence, or suppress empathy often carry those frameworks into adulthood. Some recover. Many do not. A study of former Hitler Youth members conducted decades after the war revealed lingering beliefs about racial hierarchy, national pride, and obedience to authority, despite overwhelming historical evidence of the regime's crimes. Similarly, in post-Soviet states, nostalgia for the order and clarity of youth indoctrination has surfaced among older generations. Indoctrination, once internalised, becomes not just an intellectual position but an emotional anchor—something people cling to, even when they know it was a lie.

However, the story is not always one of irreversible damage. De-radicalisation and educational reform can play a transformative role—if approached with nuance and realism. Programmes in post-Nazi Germany and post-ISIS Iraq have attempted to rebuild pluralistic curricula and offer psychological counselling to children exposed to propaganda. But success depends on recognising that indoctrination is not undone by facts alone. It must be replaced by alternative narratives—ones that offer complexity, humility, and human connection. The challenge is to construct identities that are grounded in critical thinking without leaving a void where certainty once was. Identity, after all, abhors a vacuum.

Importantly, the mechanisms of youth propaganda are not limited to overtly authoritarian regimes. Democracies too have engaged in subtle forms of nationalist education, mythologised history, and selective memory. The difference often lies in degree and transparency, not in kind. During both World Wars, British and American schools promoted patriotism and vilified enemy states. While these efforts may not have matched the systemic indoctrination of the Hitler Youth or Komsomol, they remind us that the line between education and propaganda is often drawn by intent—and erased by fear.

This invites a deeper reflection: how should societies teach history, identity, and moral values to young people in times of conflict or uncertainty? Where is the boundary between civic education and ideological imposition? These are not abstract questions. They are central to every post-conflict curriculum design, textbook reform, and national myth-making process. The danger lies not in teaching values—but in pretending they are self-evident, singular, or timeless.

Ultimately, propaganda aimed at youth is not just a strategy of war—it is a philosophy of control. It seeks to erase ambiguity, disarm empathy, and short-circuit dissent. It offers meaning without questioning, pride without context, and action without introspection. Its antidote is not only information, but education that respects complexity and nurtures the moral imagination. In that respect, the stakes are higher than we often acknowledge. For the ideas planted in young minds during conflict do not die when the war ends. They mature, mutate, and migrate into the future—carried by those who once believed them to be truth.

"Trauma Without Language":

Children do not speak trauma in paragraphs. They do not deconstruct it in analysis or articulate it in neat timelines. For many young survivors of war, genocide, and displacement, trauma is not expressed through narrative but enacted through silence, nightmares, bedwetting, sudden aggression, or compulsive repetition. Their language is not verbal but behavioural—etched into habits, drawings, posture, or play. And to miss this truth is to misread the psychology of the youngest casualties of conflict. When trauma enters a child's world, it often bypasses their ability to process it in words. But it does not go unregistered. It settles in the body, the nervous system, and the subconscious. It finds expression where language cannot reach.

In clinical psychology, this phenomenon is well-recognised. Researchers studying post-traumatic stress in child soldiers from Sierra Leone, displaced youth from Syria, and survivors of the Rwandan genocide all observe the same pattern: speech is not the child's first response to horror. Somatic symptoms—stomach aches, headaches, difficulty sleeping—emerge before articulation. Some children draw obsessively, others remain mute. One child rescued from a Burmese rebel camp spent weeks sketching only rifles and boots, over and over, without explanation. Another refused to speak at all but began lining up his toys in rows as if in military drill. What these behaviours have in common is not randomness but coherence—their own kind of logic, encoded in silence or play.

This is not unique to children in warzones. It is observable in children exposed to domestic violence, sexual abuse, or systemic neglect. But conflict amplifies the scale and frequency. In war, the trauma is not intermittent—it is daily. It is not private—it is social. And it is often layered: children lose homes, parents, structure, and language all at once. They are forced to flee, to adapt, to survive in adult situations without adult tools. The psychological impact is not a "disruption" of normal development—it is the rewriting of normal itself. The result is not just developmental delay, but identity deformation.

Traditional trauma therapy, built on verbal disclosure and narrative reprocessing, often fails to meet these children where they are. The assumption that healing begins with storytelling ignores the reality that for many children, the story is inaccessible, fragmented, or unspeakable. This has pushed the field toward more embodied and nonverbal modalities—art therapy, drama therapy, sensorimotor psychotherapy, and movement-based interventions. In refugee camps across Lebanon and Jordan, NGOs now run drawing and music sessions not as enrichment, but as triage. A child who cannot say "I am afraid" may still draw monsters with fangs or sing a song of loss in a minor key. These are not distractions. They are disclosures.

What's essential to understand is that the silence of traumatised children is not emptiness—it is intelligence. It is the nervous system's attempt to shield itself from overwhelming stimuli. It is the mind protecting the child from what the child cannot yet afford to know. Developmental psychologist Bruce Perry famously observed that "the child who flinches at every noise is not disordered—he is appropriately wired for a violent world." In other words, what may look like dysfunction is often adaptation. Behaviour must be read in context, not against the benchmark of an imagined "normal."

Silence can also be a form of protest. In post-conflict Bosnia, some children of wartime rape survivors refused to speak in public settings, despite having functional language skills. Psychologists later interpreted this as an unconscious stance against a society that denied their lineage, erased their mothers' trauma, or politicised their existence. In such cases, silence is not absence but refusal—a powerful form of embodied commentary. It says what cannot be said aloud.

There is also a cultural dimension. Western therapeutic models often privilege verbal catharsis, but in many cultures—particularly those where community over individual expression is emphasised—trauma is processed differently. In parts of Uganda and Mozambique, children formerly abducted by militias undergo traditional cleansing rituals that include dance, drumming, and storytelling by elders. These practices are not incidental—they are reparative. They restore continuity, context, and communal belonging. They allow trauma to be held not just by the child, but by the group. That collective holding is sometimes more powerful than any individual intervention.

But none of this is quick. One of the deepest misunderstandings in humanitarian psychology is the expectation of linear progress. Children may appear to improve—then regress. They may engage one day and shut down the next. Healing is not a staircase but a spiral. And it does not always end in resolution. For many children, especially those whose families remain shattered or whose communities are not rebuilt, the goal is not full recovery but functional resilience: the ability to form relationships, regulate emotion, and participate in social life. That, in itself, is a radical achievement.

The implications of this for education are significant. Classrooms become frontline spaces in the aftermath of conflict. Teachers, often untrained in trauma sensitivity, find themselves interpreting outbursts, withdrawal, or defiance without understanding their origins. A child who cannot sit still, who lashes out or disengages, is often labelled disruptive. Yet these behaviours may be the language of distress. Schools must therefore be rethought not just as sites of knowledge transmission, but as therapeutic ecosystems. Trauma-informed pedagogy—incorporating stability, routine, sensory regulation, and relational safety—is not a luxury in post-conflict zones. It is foundational.

Likewise, legal and political institutions must adapt their expectations. In courts, children may be called to testify about war crimes or atrocities. But their inability to provide linear, detailed accounts is often misread as unreliability. This is a category error. Memory under trauma is stored differently—fragmented, sensory, and often encoded in emotional rather than chronological terms. To demand adult-style coherence from a child survivor is not only unfair—it may re-traumatise them. Testimony must be reimagined, perhaps augmented by psychological interpretation, visual aids, or proxies, to honour the truth of the experience without forcing a narrative that the child cannot yet give.

What emerges from all this is a broader challenge: the need to rethink our assumptions about communication, healing, and evidence. Trauma without language is not a lesser form of suffering—it is one of the most profound. And understanding it demands more from us: more patience, more creativity, more humility. It demands that we listen not only to words, but to patterns, silences, postures, and play. That we accept expression not as a polished product, but as a raw signal—partial, symbolic, and often indirect.

Perhaps most importantly, it demands that we stop asking children to speak our language—and start learning theirs. For in the art they make, the games they play, and the rhythms they choose, something essential is communicated: that even when the world breaks, the impulse to represent it, survive it, and remake it remains intact. That impulse—before speech, before structure—is where healing begins.

Reclaiming the Future:

The aftermath of war does not end with ceasefires or treaties. For young people who have lived through the disintegration of their families, communities, and sense of safety, the end of conflict marks the beginning of another struggle: the long, often silent labour of rebuilding a sense of self, of trust, of future. Amid the ashes of conflict, the question becomes not only how to survive, but how to reclaim the capacity to imagine—and participate in—a peaceful society. It is here that rehabilitation is not merely about services or shelter. It is a deeply psychological and cultural project. And increasingly, it is youth who carry its most fragile but transformative potential.

At the heart of effective post-conflict recovery is a recognition that young survivors are not merely passive recipients of aid but essential agents in shaping a sustainable peace. Programmes developed by UNICEF and similar institutions have evolved beyond basic humanitarian triage. They now aim to repair not only the physical damage of war, but the psychic architecture of childhood itself. This includes education initiatives, vocational training, and psychosocial support—but also, crucially, space for narrative agency. In post-conflict zones from Colombia to South Sudan, storytelling workshops, participatory media projects, and youth-led theatre have become as central to recovery as food distribution or vaccination drives. The premise is simple yet profound: telling one's story is not a luxury. It is a form of re-entry into civic life.

Take, for example, the Child Friendly Spaces set up by UNICEF in eastern Democratic Republic of Congo. These are not traditional classrooms. They are safe zones where displaced and traumatised children gather to draw, play, and—when ready—talk. Facilitators trained in child psychology create structured opportunities for expression: through murals, puppet shows, songs, and sometimes just unstructured play. In one programme, children were given disposable cameras to photograph their surroundings. The resulting images were not technically refined, but they captured something essential: glimpses of ruined homes, mothers cooking under tarps, siblings asleep on dirt floors. One boy's photo of his bare feet next to an unexploded mortar shell said more than any report. These expressions are not merely cathartic. They are diagnostic. They tell aid workers what children notice, remember, fear, and hope for.

The shift from silence to story—especially in young survivors of sexual violence or combat—is not just an emotional arc. It is a political one. In Sierra Leone, former child soldiers enrolled in reintegration programmes often faced intense stigma from their communities. Traditional rites of purification, where available, helped. But the deeper transformation came when these youth began documenting their own experiences through radio dramas and public dialogue forums. Telling the truth, on their own terms, began to rehumanise them—not only in the eyes of their neighbours, but in their own. This is not merely about trauma disclosure. It is about authorship. When young people are permitted to speak as subjects of their own histories—not just as objects of pity or policy—they reassert their place in society.

This process is fragile, and fraught. Not every society embraces these stories. In Sri Lanka, young Tamils who experienced the civil war as children faced institutional erasure of their narratives in state-controlled curricula. Where memory is politically inconvenient, storytelling itself becomes a site of resistance. But even in repressive contexts, underground initiatives often emerge. In Myanmar, despite censorship, youth art collectives have documented the country's cycles of violence through graffiti, poetry, and zines circulated by hand. These creative outlets are not fringe—they are civic rehearsal. They teach collaboration, empathy, and public voice.

The therapeutic value of storytelling has long been recognised. But what is emerging now is a broader appreciation for its civic function. In Rwanda, post-genocide reconciliation was supported not only by formal mechanisms like Gacaca courts, but also by youth storytelling circles supported by local NGOs. These were not tribunals. They were places where young people—both survivors and perpetrators—could narrate their experiences, express remorse, and explore moral grey zones. A boy who admitted to participating in killings because "it was the only way to avoid being killed" was not excused—but he was heard. These spaces introduced a different kind of justice: restorative rather than retributive, relational rather than abstract.

Critics argue that these interventions risk instrumentalising children's pain—that storytelling becomes just another tool in the donor development toolkit. But this critique misses the point. Youth storytelling is not only about individual healing; it is about constructing a shared moral memory. Societies that suppress the voices of war-affected youth tend to repeat their violence. Societies that listen—and adapt—are more likely to develop inclusive civic institutions. This is not sentimentalism. It is evidenced in comparative peace-building research from transitional justice scholars across Latin America and Africa.

The most compelling programmes allow youth to shape the format as well as the content of their storytelling. In Colombia, Fundación Mi Sangre supports former child soldiers to create digital comics based on their experiences, blending autobiography with metaphor and fiction. This creative distance enables them to explore trauma without becoming re-traumatised. In Uganda, the Refugee Law Project has helped young refugees develop community radio shows, reaching rural populations with narratives that challenge stigma and offer models of resilience. These initiatives work not because they are expressive, but because they are reciprocal. They allow youth to participate not just in testimony, but in the redesign of the public sphere.

Importantly, the future-orientation of such programmes distinguishes them from trauma therapies that remain fixated on the past. Reclaiming the future means imagining it—and then equipping young people with the tools, roles, and responsibilities to build it. This includes leadership training, civic education, and mentorship. But it also involves something harder to measure: trust. When institutions invite youth to co-create their post-conflict society—rather than treating them solely as victims—they signal a shift in relational power. The child is no longer merely protected by the state. They are shaping it.

This is not a one-size-fits-all solution. The cultural, historical, and political context matters immensely. What is possible in post-genocide Rwanda may not work in post-civil war Yemen. But across cases, one pattern recurs: where young people are silenced, peace remains brittle. Where they are engaged, peace becomes durable—not because youth are innately virtuous, but because they are the demographic majority and moral barometer of the post-war generation.

What emerges from this landscape is a redefinition of rehabilitation. It is not about returning children to a pre-war innocence—that innocence is gone. It is about enabling them to narrate and negotiate their place in a world still marked by violence, complexity, and moral ambiguity. This requires listening not only with compassion, but with rigour. Their stories are not simply emotional accounts. They are strategic blueprints for the kind of society that can survive after catastrophe.

The long arc of peace does not bend on policy alone. It is bent by voices—often young, often unpolished—that insist on being heard. And when those voices tell stories not only of what was lost, but of what might still be made, they do more than reclaim the future. They begin to author it.

Chapter 7
The Shadow Self of Civilization: War as Humanity's Mirror

Civilisation likes to think of itself as an ever-upward climb—layer upon layer of law, ethics, diplomacy, and social restraint. Yet the moment war ignites, these fine constructions often prove paper-thin. Rules are suspended. Masks slip. The comforting notion of steady moral progress gives way to something rawer, harder to face: war is not merely civilisation's undoing, but its unmasking. In the furnace of conflict, societies meet not only their external foes, but the buried and disowned parts of their own psyche. This is the encounter at the heart of this chapter—not with some distant adversary, but with humanity's own contradictions, staring back.

We tend to tell the story of war through manoeuvres, treaties, and outcomes. Beneath those visible threads, though, runs a deeper weave: the psychological repetitions that echo through centuries. When Homer depicted Achilles dragging Hector's corpse behind his chariot, he wasn't simply noting a gruesome flourish of vengeance. He was naming something that happens again and again, on every continent—the human drive to strip an enemy of their humanity, to turn a person into a symbol to be humiliated or destroyed. From Troy's dust to Verdun's trenches, war has shown less about collapse than about exposure: who we become when freed from consequence. And the face we see in that moment is rarely alien—it is alarmingly recognisable.

Hannah Arendt captured this unsettling familiarity with unusual clarity when she reported on Adolf Eichmann's 1961 trial. Eichmann was no raving sadist, no zealot frothing with ideology. He was, chillingly, a bureaucrat: polite in manner, diligent in execution, incurious about the moral weight of his work. Arendt's phrase—"the banality of evil"—provoked such unease precisely because it broke apart the comfortable belief that only monsters commit monstrous acts. Since then, from Rwanda to Bosnia to the cells of Abu Ghraib, we have seen the same truth unfold: atrocity is often carried out not by aberrations, but by people who see themselves as dutiful, even righteous. They process forms. They follow orders. They complete their shift. The horror lies not in their madness, but in their normality.

Here, Carl Jung's notion of the "shadow" becomes instructive. In his framework, the shadow is that part of the self we push away—envy, cruelty, aggression, fear. In peacetime, such impulses are contained, disguised, projected outward. War, however, rips away those restraints. It doesn't just allow the shadow to emerge; it crowns it leader. The enemy becomes the vessel for everything we cannot bear to acknowledge in ourselves. In this way, war is more than a matter of territory or politics—it is a theatre for projection, a ritual meant to purge the parts of ourselves we dare not claim, by destroying them in others. And in legitimising that act, war dignifies the outward expression of the inner demon.

This helps explain why some societies feel drawn to war—not in spite of its horror, but because of its heightened intensity. In times of uncertainty, there is a kind of seduction in extremes, a bracing simplicity in the collapse of complexity into binaries: us and them, right and wrong, order and chaos. This appeal is not the sole preserve of tyrants. Even liberal democracies have flirted with purifying rhetoric—whether through drone campaigns, sweeping surveillance, or nationalist revivals. The myth of war as crucible—burning away weakness, forging identity—retains its pull. In its most dangerous telling, war becomes not tragedy to avert, but a cleansing flame to be welcomed.

Yet focusing only on the architects of war misses its pervasiveness. War's logic seeps into the language, the habits, the assumptions of everyday life. Its mental architecture—binary thinking ("with us or against us"), selective empathy (mourning our dead but not theirs), moral self-exemption ("we had no choice"), sanitising euphemism ("collateral damage," "enhanced interrogation")—is not conjured from nothing. These patterns already exist, in milder form, in playground disputes, office politics, online skirmishes. Wartime merely scales them up. The seeds are sown long before the uniforms are donned.

And so we arrive at one of the most unsettling recognitions: the inner tyrant. The potential to rationalise cruelty exists in all of us. It doesn't need ideology—only a justification, a fear, a sense of belonging. War institutionalises these rationalisations, but they germinate quietly within the soil of ordinary life. The soldier who dehumanises a foe shares a certain mental kinship with the co-worker who scapegoats a colleague, or the citizen who explains away the suffering of refugees. The leap from petty exclusion to sanctioned violence is less a chasm than a slope.

There is, however, an opposing force—one that is hard, deliberate, and fragile. Facing the shadow, whether in a person or a nation, is not something that happens by accident. It demands introspection, humility, and, above all, restraint. Post-war reconciliation efforts often falter not because of technical failings, but because they skirt the confrontation with complicity. Germany's long process of *Vergangenheitsbewältigung*—its public reckoning with the Nazi past—stands as a rare attempt to do that work at a national scale. Through education, memorials, and open dialogue, the country worked to embed a sobering lesson: evil is not an aberration, but a possibility within the ordinary. The aim was not purification, but vigilance. Civilisation's task is not to erase the capacity for violence, but to recognise it—and to keep it bound.

This chapter is not a march through battles past. It is, instead, a mirror. Drawing on ancient epics, legal archives, psychological insight, and philosophical inquiry, it will explore how war throws the human psyche into stark relief. The intent is neither to romanticise nor to reduce war to pathology, but to read it as a diagnostic—an X-ray of civilisation's skeleton, showing both its endurance and its cracks. From Homer to Arendt to Jung, from the hills of Troy to the ruins of modern conflict, the lesson repeats: the line dividing civilisation from barbarism does not run along borders. It cuts through each individual.

To read on is to accept a certain discomfort: the capacity for ruin lives not in some distant stranger, but in the architecture of the everyday mind. Yet it is also to accept an invitation—to look steadily at that shadow, to resist the temptation of denial, and to imagine a peace that does not rest on illusions, but on maturity of mind. Peace, in this light, is not simply the silencing of guns, but the steady practice of containment—the ongoing, deliberate management of the shadow. And perhaps, more than any treaty or political accord, it is this discipline that marks the true measure of civilisation.

Echoes from the Ancient World:

The idea that war reveals something essential about human nature is not new. Homer understood this more than two thousand years ago. *The Iliad*, composed in the eighth century BCE, is not a glorification of victory but a deep meditation on rage, honour, grief, and the psychology of killing. Achilles, the poem's central figure, is not merely a warrior; he is a study in wounded pride, existential confusion, and the volatility of the human ego under extreme conditions. His emotional spiral—triggered by the loss of a companion, the insult of a superior, and the existential weight of mortality—mirrors the very dynamics we continue to witness in modern conflict zones, whether among foot soldiers in Iraq or drone operators thousands of miles from the battlefield. *The core emotions of war—humiliation, vengeance, fear, righteousness—have not evolved. What has changed is only their technological expression.*

This continuity in psychological response across eras invites serious scrutiny. Despite radical shifts in military hardware, command structures, and international law, the internal landscape of the combatant remains astonishingly stable. The Roman legions, Napoleon's conscripts, and America's Marines have all carried within them the same constellation of motivations and contradictions. Even when the rhetoric around war changes—democracy, divine will, national security—the emotional architecture tends to echo ancient templates. The soldier's fear of death, the rush of camaraderie, the disorienting sense of moral dislocation—all of these appear in both Homeric poetry and post-deployment psychiatric assessments. *The fact that the Iliad still resonates is not a testament to Homer's genius alone, but to the uncomfortable persistence of human psychological patterns under duress.*

One particularly instructive comparison lies in the portrayal of glory. In *The Iliad*, glory (*kleos*) is existential currency. It grants a kind of immortality that physical death cannot erase. Achilles knows that he will die young if he fights, yet he also knows that withdrawing from battle will render his name irrelevant. This tragic calculus still governs many modern decisions about risk, sacrifice, and identity. Today's combatants may not invoke the Muses, but they are shaped by powerful narratives of legacy, honour, and belonging. Whether through military medals, public funerals, or commemorative documentaries, the contemporary world still elevates certain deaths as *meaningful. The moral architecture of heroism remains structurally intact—only the aesthetic and ideological language around it has changed.*

At the same time, Homer does not sentimentalise violence. He dwells on it, anatomically and emotionally. Warriors die not in glory but in agony, their bodies described in visceral, almost clinical terms. The narrative invites pity, not triumphalism. This is not unlike the better reporting from modern conflict zones, where war correspondents focus not on strategic gains but on civilian casualties, medical trauma, and the psychological toll. That such portrayals continue to clash with state-sponsored narratives of precision, control, and moral clarity reveals a persistent tension: the truth of war is often at odds with its public justification. *From Homer to the present, there has always been a disjunction between the experience of war and the stories told about it.*

Moreover, Homer's understanding of the emotional instability of soldiers anticipates modern psychological diagnoses. Achilles, in his grief and rage, withdraws from society, exhibits irrational aggression, and enters a kind of dissociative state. Contemporary combat veterans suffering from PTSD often report similar patterns—emotional numbness, outbursts of violence, difficulty reintegrating into civilian life. But even more telling is the moral injury Achilles suffers. He does not lose his mind; he loses his moral compass. After killing Hector, he mutilates his body and drags it in the dirt, not for strategic advantage, but out of wounded pride and dehumanised fury. Such acts, and the psychological collapse that follows, are documented not just in ancient epic but in modern war crimes tribunals and soldiers' memoirs. *What Homer teaches us is that moral injury is not a modern pathology—it is a timeless consequence of crossing certain psychological thresholds in combat.*

Equally relevant is the theme of authority and its corruptions. Agamemnon, the Greek commander, is not a noble leader but a manipulative politician who provokes dissent, abuses power, and sacrifices his own men's morale for ego. This too feels contemporary. The disconnect between military command and ground realities, the tension between political imperatives and ethical responsibility, recurs in nearly every modern war. From Vietnam to Afghanistan, from the trenches of World War I to the bureaucratic miscalculations of Iraq, we see the same dynamics: leaders who speak of honour while withholding adequate support, soldiers who follow orders with diminishing faith, and a public that alternates between adulation and abandonment. *Homer's war is political theatre intertwined with human tragedy—a pairing that remains disturbingly familiar.*

Even the portrayal of the enemy in *The Iliad* demonstrates psychological nuance often missing in modern military discourse. Hector, the Trojan prince, is not demonised. He is dignified, courageous, and tragically human. His final moments are not rendered as a triumph for the Greeks but as a moment of profound sorrow. This capacity to humanise the enemy stands in stark contrast to many modern propaganda systems, which often rely on caricature, dehumanisation, and the erasure of individual complexity. Yet when modern combat veterans speak candidly, they often express an eerie recognition of their adversaries—not just as threats, but as mirror images: young, frightened, uncertain. *Homer's enemy is not a monster. He is simply a man who happens to be standing on the other side.*

It is worth asking, then: if the psychological grammar of war is so persistent, what does this imply for our models of peace? Much of contemporary peacebuilding assumes that war is a deviation from the norm, a rupture that can be repaired by re-establishing order, democracy, or infrastructure. But Homer suggests that war is not an anomaly. It is a deeply human response to fear, honour, shame, and mortality. To prevent war—or to heal from it—requires not just policy changes but a reckoning with these deeper drivers. *Peace cannot be engineered only through treaties; it must be cultivated through psychological awareness.*

That is perhaps why ancient texts endure: they do not flatter the reader with illusions of progress. They expose continuity. And in doing so, they offer something rare in modern discourse—a lens for humility. When we read about the rage of Achilles or the sorrow of Priam, who begs for his son's body, we are not encountering archaic emotions. We are encountering ourselves. The enduring power of these stories lies in their refusal to simplify, to excuse, or to resolve. *They demand that we see war not as a break from civilisation, but as a disclosure of what civilisation keeps at bay.*

By tracing the emotional contours of warfare from Bronze Age epics to drone warfare, we come to a sobering conclusion: the technologies have evolved, but the human mind has not kept pace. If anything, our capacity for abstraction—through bureaucratic systems, remote warfare, and ideological distancing—has made it easier to commit ancient cruelties with modern efficiency. *We still bleed for honour, kill for belonging, and grieve with the same bewildered silence.*

What the ancient world offers is not a blueprint for modern conduct, but a mirror. And in that mirror, if we are honest, we can see the psychological infrastructure that sustains both violence and its rationalisations. To read Homer today is not to indulge in literary nostalgia. It is to conduct an audit of human tendencies—to locate the fault lines, the impulses, the unacknowledged drives. And perhaps, to start thinking about how we might interrupt them. Not through moralising, but through understanding. Not by pretending we are different, but by recognising how little has changed—and why that matters.

The Banality of Evil Revisited:

It was not the face of a monster that shocked Hannah Arendt at the 1961 trial of Adolf Eichmann. It was the face of a bureaucrat—ordinary, mild-mannered, maddeningly banal. Eichmann, one of the principal organisers of the Holocaust, did not present as a man possessed by hatred or grand ideology. He insisted he was merely following orders, obeying laws, performing administrative duties. To Arendt, this was more chilling than overt sadism. Evil, she argued, is often not committed by demonic figures but by disturbingly normal people operating within systems that reward obedience and punish moral reflection. *The banality of evil*, a term she coined, was not a claim that evil acts are trivial; rather, it was a warning that *the most horrific crimes can be committed without malice, when individuals abdicate moral agency in favour of procedural conformity.*

More than sixty years later, her thesis is not only relevant—it may be indispensable. From drone warfare operators to border patrol agents, from intelligence analysts approving torture protocols to tech contractors writing software for authoritarian regimes, we are surrounded by modern-day Eichmanns: individuals who do not set policy but execute it, often at arm's length from its human consequences. Unlike caricatured villains, these actors rarely relish cruelty. They operate under metrics, checklists, career incentives, and ideological abstractions. Their evil is neither explosive nor theatrical. It is quiet, cumulative, procedural. And it thrives in the hollowed-out spaces where ethics should reside.

Consider the My Lai massacre in Vietnam, 1968. American soldiers systematically murdered over 500 unarmed civilians, including children and elderly villagers. The chain of command failed catastrophically at every level. But what stands out is not just the horror of the acts but the stunning normalcy of the perpetrators. Many were young conscripts, trained not in cruelty but in dehumanisation. In court, some insisted they were merely following orders. Others claimed confusion, fear, or the psychological inertia of group behaviour. What emerged was not a portrait of psychopathic hatred, but of moral disengagement—of otherwise unremarkable individuals swept into atrocity through institutional logic, peer pressure, and the subtle erosion of ethical guardrails.

Fast-forward to Abu Ghraib, 2003. Photographs of American military police abusing Iraqi detainees—stripping them naked, hooding them, stacking them into human pyramids—shocked the global public. Yet those involved were not trained torturers. They were reservists, corrections officers, and clerks. The defence mounted by many echoed Eichmann's: they were following protocol, responding to vague instructions from higher-ups, encouraged by a culture of impunity and ambiguous legality. The scandal revealed not only individual failings but systemic rot—policies designed to avoid accountability, bureaucratic language engineered to sanitise cruelty, and an institutional tolerance for moral ambiguity so long as it produced "results."

The technology of modern warfare has only deepened these dilemmas. A drone pilot stationed in Nevada may kill targets in Yemen with clinical precision—never seeing the aftermath, never meeting the dead. The disconnection is profound. The language is euphemistic: "target acquisition," "kinetic action," "collateral damage." This is not simply jargon; it is psychological insulation. The more complex and mediated the system, the easier it becomes for individuals to retreat from personal responsibility. *When violence is operationalised through screens and acronyms, the moral costs can vanish behind the dashboard.*

Arendt's warning about moral thoughtlessness is precisely what makes this structure so dangerous. Evil does not always require hatred; it requires detachment. When every act is broken down into fragments—authorised by one, executed by another, justified by a third—the ethical weight is diffused across a system. And when that system rewards efficiency over reflection, compliance over conscience, the results can be catastrophic. *This is how crimes against humanity can unfold without a single person waking up in the morning intending to do evil.*

Contemporary regimes have mastered this architecture. In China's Xinjiang province, the mass internment of Uyghur Muslims is facilitated not by sadistic tyrants but by data analysts, surveillance engineers, transport managers, and regional officials. Camps are designed, built, staffed, and maintained not in secret but as part of a state apparatus. Language is sanitised—reeducation centres, vocational training, national unity. The reality, of course, is forced assimilation, psychological trauma, and cultural erasure. But the bureaucratic face of the operation—mundane, spreadsheet-driven, clothed in legality—makes resistance difficult and culpability diffuse. The system absorbs dissent not by silencing individuals but by reducing them to functionaries within an impersonal process.

The same logic animated the post-genocide apparatus in Rwanda, where thousands of perpetrators—often neighbours of their victims—participated in massacres that were horrifying in scale and disturbingly intimate. Many later claimed they had been swept up by collective fear, propaganda, and the disintegration of social norms. The Gacaca courts, a grassroots justice mechanism, attempted to unearth truth and assign responsibility, but the psychological terrain remained murky. *What emerges from these cases is not only the horror of violence but the fragility of moral identity when embedded within institutions that reward conformity and suppress reflection.*

And yet, Arendt's critics have rightly pointed out that the concept of *banality* should not obscure the role of ideology, power, or choice. Eichmann was not simply a cog in a machine; he actively pursued promotions, manipulated rules, and demonstrated chilling ingenuity in organising deportations. Bureaucrats are not neutral instruments. They have agency. The danger lies in how that agency becomes constrained—socially, institutionally, psychologically—until it feels irrelevant. The modern tragedy is not that individuals are coerced into evil, but that *they can convince themselves they are not doing evil at all.*

This raises urgent questions about responsibility. If evil can be banal, what prevents us from becoming complicit? What ethical training prepares people to resist dehumanising systems? Traditional models of moral education—religion, civic duty, personal virtue—seem inadequate in the face of complex, diffuse bureaucracies. Whistleblowers and conscientious objectors are often ostracised or punished. Institutions reward loyalty, not introspection. The courage to say "no" to systemic wrongs often arises not from formal ethics but from inner conviction—what Arendt called "thinking without a banister." *It is the act of moral imagination—of seeing the human consequences behind procedural language—that forms the last line of defence against bureaucratised evil.*

Education, then, must do more than impart rules. It must cultivate psychological resilience, ethical ambiguity, and the courage to dissent. The stories of those who refused to participate—Sergeant Hugh Thompson in My Lai, who intervened to stop the massacre; Albert Battel, the Wehrmacht officer who defied Nazi orders to protect Jews—show that resistance is possible. But it requires a deliberate rejection of moral laziness. It requires individuals to see systems clearly—and to resist the temptation to retreat into their folds.

Today's world is awash in systems that depersonalise: algorithmic governance, technocratic policy, outsourced violence. Each promises efficiency. Each risks the erosion of responsibility. Arendt's great insight was that evil need not be spectacular to be devastating. It can wear a tie, fill out forms, speak in technical jargon. *Its danger lies in its ordinariness—in how easily we accept its logic when it is camouflaged in administrative routine.*

This is not a pessimistic conclusion. It is a call to vigilance. To understand evil as banal is not to excuse it, but to expose it. It strips away the myth that atrocity belongs only to monsters. It demands that we examine the systems we inhabit, the roles we play, the thoughts we refuse to think. It insists that ethics is not a trait we possess, but a habit we practise—especially when no one is watching. Arendt's legacy is not a theory of despair. It is a philosophy of responsibility in an age of abstraction. And it begins with the most radical of acts: *thinking.*

The Seduction of the Apocalyptic:

War is often framed as a failure of diplomacy, a collapse of civil order, or the tragic outgrowth of geopolitical tension. Yet history compels us to consider a darker, more psychologically unsettling possibility: that for some individuals and societies, war is not merely endured but desired. Not despite its destructiveness—but *because of* it. The brutality of war, in this reading, is seductive precisely because it burns away ambiguity, simplifies moral landscapes, and momentarily suspends the complex weight of civilian life. It creates what Carl Jung might call a *clarifying extremity*—a theatre in which the hidden parts of the psyche, long suppressed by civilisation, are given free rein. To understand this drive, we must examine not just strategy or ideology, but the psychological shadow that modernity tries, and often fails, to repress.

Jung's concept of the "shadow" refers to the unconscious repository of the parts of ourselves we deny, fear, or deem incompatible with our self-image—impulses toward rage, cruelty, dominance, vengeance. In individuals, repressing this shadow may produce a brittle persona, outwardly civilised but inwardly fragile. In collectives, the effects can be explosive. Nations too have shadows: unacknowledged traumas, racial resentments, ideological puritanism, and historical grievances buried under the polished rhetoric of unity and progress. When stress mounts or identity is threatened, the shadow erupts—not always in sudden violence, but in a cumulative slide toward extremism, scapegoating, and, ultimately, militarisation.

There is a reason fascist regimes are often drawn to the aesthetics of apocalypse. Mussolini's speeches were laced with references to war as a purifying fire; Hitler's *Mein Kampf* framed conflict as biologically and morally redemptive. In the rhetoric of ISIS, destruction is not a consequence of divine mission—it *is* the divine mission. The impulse here is not strictly tactical. It is spiritual, even ecstatic. In a world perceived as weak, decadent, and morally compromised, war is mythologised as a cleansing act. A way to destroy not just the enemy, but ambiguity itself. It is this psychological function of war—as a tool to collapse complexity—that makes it so enduringly tempting.

Modern liberal societies tend to frame peace as the highest good. But peace is difficult. It demands tolerance, compromise, and an uncomfortable coexistence with difference and uncertainty. In contrast, war offers moral certainty. It divides the world into good and evil, us and them, cleanly and with conviction. This binary is deeply appealing—particularly in moments of national anxiety, economic instability, or cultural upheaval. Leaders who promise clarity in the face of chaos often invoke martial imagery not for its policy relevance but for its psychological charge. The war on terror. The war on drugs. The war on wokeism. Each is a metaphor, but not a harmless one. Beneath it lies a deeper yearning: to escape nuance, to surrender complexity, and to be *right* without having to question oneself.

This is why apocalyptic narratives thrive not only in failed states but also in stable democracies. They appear in populist movements, conspiratorial subcultures, and even in entertainment. Consider the popularity of post-apocalyptic films and novels—not merely as escapism, but as speculative wish-fulfilment. The fantasy of a world-ending event is often less about survival than liberation. From taxes, from bureaucracy, from moral grey zones. In this light, it is not just despots who crave the apocalypse; it is the disillusioned citizen, the humiliated patriot, the anxious ideologue. *The desire is not for death itself, but for the death of ambiguity.*

There are echoes of this in the United States' invasion of Iraq in 2003. While official justifications ranged from weapons of mass destruction to humanitarian intervention, the cultural subtext was strikingly mythic. It was a war framed in terms of moral reckoning, existential confrontation, and a reassertion of American will. What was obscured was the banality of the real enemy: uncertainty. Intelligence failures, geopolitical nuance, sectarian complexity—these had no place in the post-9/11 narrative architecture. What prevailed was a craving to *do something*, to reassert clarity through force. And the consequences were catastrophic.

Russia's war in Ukraine presents a different iteration of the same psychology. Vladimir Putin's appeals to imperial restoration and metaphysical destiny are not rooted in geopolitical rationalism but in civilisational mythology. His war is not about tangible security threats, but about resurrecting a lost grandeur, purging weakness, and reasserting an identity that cannot tolerate modern pluralism. For the regime, and for many of its supporters, war is not an unfortunate necessity. It is the *stage upon which the shadow can dance unashamed.* That it costs thousands of lives is not a deterrent; it is part of the spectacle.

Understanding the seduction of the apocalyptic demands a hard look at democratic societies as well. It is easy to locate this pathology in dictatorships. It is harder to see how it seeps into the cracks of democratic life—through the cult of the strongman, the romance of armed rebellion, or the fetishisation of national crisis. Even peacekeeping institutions are not immune. The deployment of force under the flag of international order often functions as a symbolic reaffirmation of moral clarity. That such interventions are frequently ambiguous in outcome, or compromised in implementation, rarely diminishes their appeal in the public imagination. *What matters, psychologically, is not success, but the performance of decisiveness.*

Carl Jung warned that confronting the shadow was essential not to eliminate it, but to integrate it. To acknowledge the darker parts of human nature—aggression, fear, domination—without letting them dominate us. Societies that fail to do this externalise their darkness, projecting it onto enemies, inventing threats, creating ritualised violence to maintain internal coherence. The temptation of war becomes the temptation of the mirror: to destroy the Other in order to avoid seeing oneself. This is why the apocalypse is seductive. It promises not just the end of the world, but the end of doubt.

There are counterforces, of course. Truth commissions, peacebuilding institutions, interfaith dialogues, civic education—all attempt to reintegrate the shadow through speech rather than blood. But these efforts require stamina, imagination, and above all, the humility to live without the illusion of perfect clarity. They are not dramatic. They are not seductive. And they rarely command the same attention as the clarion call of war. But they may be the only antidote to its allure.

In the final analysis, the question is not why some leaders and societies are drawn to war. The question is why so many others are not. For war offers something deeply human: the illusion of simplicity, the rush of purpose, the license to act without introspection. It is a dangerous gift. But understanding it is not an act of indulgence. It is a necessity. *Because until we confront the parts of ourselves that crave destruction, we will remain vulnerable to those who promise to deliver it in our name.*

Facing the Inner Tyrant:

It is easy to locate tyranny in others. History makes villains accessible, their atrocities preserved in court transcripts, documentaries, and school textbooks. We condemn their violence, their fanaticism, their capacity to rationalise horror. But the harder, more uncomfortable question is this: *What part of that logic lives quietly within us?* What if tyranny is not only a condition of the world but also a latent tendency of the human psyche? The psychology of wartime cruelty—how people justify harm, abdicate moral responsibility, or turn silence into complicity—is not exclusive to generals and guards. It emerges, in subtler form, in daily decisions, social institutions, and interior monologues. To confront it fully, we must face what Carl Jung called the "inner tyrant": that aspect of ourselves which seeks dominance, control, and moral superiority at the expense of others.

War does not invent this impulse. It merely amplifies it. Under pressure, the human mind reaches for shortcuts: binary distinctions, tribal loyalty, and moral licensing. The psychological mechanisms that enable violence in wartime—dehumanisation, projection, euphemistic labelling—have close cousins in civilian life. Take, for example, how we describe enemy combatants versus victims. "Collateral damage" is a phrase designed not to lie but to *anaesthetise.* It creates moral distance. Likewise, the bureaucratic language of wartime logistics—the numbers, metrics, and classifications—has the effect of reducing complex human realities to operational abstractions. This is not limited to battlefields. It happens in corporate boardrooms, immigration systems, and social media platforms, where algorithmic sorting can mask structural harm. *The danger is not in intention, but in the quiet ease with which justification displaces empathy.*

Hannah Arendt's insight into the "banality of evil" remains critical here. Her observation of Adolf Eichmann revealed not a monster but a functionary—a man who claimed to be simply doing his job, following orders, deferring judgment to higher authorities. This raises a disturbing question: how many of us, in certain contexts, would behave the same? Not because we are inherently cruel, but because we are trained—often unconsciously—to value rules, roles, and results over ethical reflection. The capacity to externalise blame is a deeply human defence mechanism. It shields the self from cognitive dissonance. "I was just trying to protect my family." "I didn't make the policy." "That's just how the system works." These rationalisations are not evil in isolation. But when stacked, reinforced, and institutionalised, they create conditions in which atrocities can be normalised. *Tyranny thrives not on brutality alone, but on the ordinary refusal to see.*

The field of moral psychology offers useful insight. Research into moral disengagement, as developed by psychologist Albert Bandura, outlines how individuals dissociate from the consequences of their actions by restructuring them cognitively. Soldiers might frame killing as duty, civilians as subhuman, orders as sacred. In civilian contexts, this mechanism appears in how we explain away discrimination, corporate exploitation, or environmental harm. The justification may not be aggressive, but it is often defensively self-soothing. "It's just business." "They should try harder." "That's not my problem." Here again, the inner tyrant does not shout; it whispers.

A related pattern is projection—the displacement of one's own unacceptable traits or fears onto others. In times of national stress, leaders often capitalise on this by constructing enemies that mirror internal anxieties. Immigrants become symbols of disorder. Activists become threats to tradition. Foreigners are blamed for domestic failure. These narratives offer relief by externalising complexity. They convert self-examination into scapegoating. On a personal level, projection appears in everyday conflict: the colleague we resent because they remind us of our own ambition, the partner we accuse of coldness to mask our own detachment. This is not melodrama; it is the psychology of avoidance. *To deny the shadow within, we cast it outward.*

One of the most powerful tools of the inner tyrant is moral exceptionalism—the belief that "we" are inherently more just, more advanced, or more entitled than "they" are. This belief, often couched in nationalist or ideological terms, provides a framework for harm that feels righteous. It is the moral fuel behind wars of liberation that devolve into occupation, peacekeeping missions that drift into domination. But this same exceptionalism appears at the individual level when we justify double standards, manipulate outcomes, or bend ethics in the service of self-interest. "I had no choice." "They deserved it." "I was protecting something more important." These are not necessarily lies; they are narratives designed to preserve identity.

What distinguishes the tyrant within from ordinary self-interest is not just ambition but the refusal to engage with inconvenient truths. Tyranny is fed by certainty—moral, ideological, emotional. When individuals or groups become so certain of their own virtue that doubt is cast as betrayal, dialogue becomes impossible. This is how families fracture, institutions harden, and societies polarise. The inability to hold competing truths, to admit error without collapse, is a core vulnerability. In wartime, this dynamic becomes deadly. In peacetime, it corrodes relationships, policy, and public discourse.

Authoritarianism does not begin at the ballot box. It begins in the psyche—when questioning is replaced by righteousness.

There are, of course, antidotes. Self-awareness, cultivated through reflection, dialogue, and education, allows individuals to recognise their own biases and limitations. But awareness alone is not sufficient. What is needed is *moral stamina*—the capacity to remain in discomfort, to resist the urge to resolve tension prematurely through blame or retreat. This is difficult work. It means confronting our own role in systems of harm, our silence when speaking might have mattered, our complicity in outcomes we privately regret. But this is the work of liberation—not from others, but from the unconscious dynamics that distort our judgment.

The rehabilitation of post-conflict societies often hinges on this kind of reckoning. South Africa's Truth and Reconciliation Commission, for all its flaws, aimed not just to punish wrongdoers but to bring private truths into public discourse. This model, though contextually unique, illustrates a broader principle: that healing requires a confrontation with the self. It is not enough to change laws or leaders. Without psychological integration—acknowledging what was denied, spoken and unspoken—cycles of violence simply mutate and return. The same principle applies to individuals. Therapy, education, even honest conversation, are tools not just for growth but for *containment*—so that the inner tyrant is not allowed to roam unchecked.

We cannot eliminate the tyrant within. But we can make it visible. We can notice its strategies: when we dehumanise, when we deflect, when we simplify the complex for the sake of comfort. We can develop the discipline to ask hard questions: What am I refusing to see? Whom have I decided not to care about? What narrative am I using to excuse myself? These questions are not punitive; they are emancipatory. They allow us to become less reactive, more just, more human.

To study war is not only to study armies, doctrines, or ideologies. It is to study the human mind under pressure—its brilliance, its delusions, its capacity for both courage and cruelty. By tracing the logics that drive wartime behaviour back into the rhythms of ordinary life, we gain not just insight but agency. We are no longer passive inheritors of violence. We become stewards of its prevention.

The inner tyrant thrives in silence. It fears reflection. And it survives in all of us—not as a monster, but as an impulse. To rule, to avoid, to dominate. Its defeat is not theatrical. It is daily, psychological, incremental. And it begins the moment we choose to see it.

Chapter 8
Strategy of the Soul: Applying Wartime Wisdom to Civilian Life

War has always served as a brutal but unflinching mirror, stripping away pretence and forcing decisions that can redirect the course of history. In its most condensed hours, it tests not only the strength of armies but the architecture of human values—probing the limits of endurance, precision of thought, and, at times, the depths of compassion. For all its savagery, war has been a severe tutor. This is the paradox we shy away from: while civilisations strive towards peace, some of the most enduring insights into leadership, psychology, timing, and moral judgement have been forged in the crucible of conflict. The teachings of generals, resistance leaders, and intelligence operatives spill well beyond the battlefield, into the unruly terrain of everyday crises: moments when leaders falter, ethics blur, strategies fail, and the balance between haste and caution hangs by a thread. Filtered through wisdom rather than violence, the logic of war can become a compass for navigating complexity in civilian life.

To suggest that we might draw lessons from war is neither a romantic indulgence nor a cynical manoeuvre—it is a pragmatic recognition. From Sun Tzu to Clausewitz to modern strategists, the most lucid military minds have insisted that war is rarely about brute force; it is the disciplined orchestration of foresight, adaptability, and control when certainty is impossible. These same faculties prove essential in arenas far removed from gunfire: diplomacy, business, parenting, community work, personal transformation. After all, "conflict" may just as easily be a negotiation, a domestic dispute, a moral reckoning, or a battle with one's own fears. What is learned in the fire remains relevant anywhere stakes are high and clarity elusive.

Take timing. Perhaps the most underestimated virtue in both war and life is patience—not the idle kind, but an active, deliberate restraint. The guerrilla fighters of Vietnam and Afghanistan mastered this, prevailing not through overwhelming firepower but through waiting—striking only when the conditions, psychological and material, tipped in their favour. Cold War tacticians, too, operated on a calculus of nerves as much as numbers. The Cuban Missile Crisis is remembered less for what happened than for what did not—because each delay, each carefully timed message, altered the path of history. Centuries earlier, Sun Tzu observed that "he who is prudent and lies in wait for an enemy who is not, will be victorious." The principle applies whether the opponent is a rival army, a collapsing market, or a fraught conversation: sometimes, the bravest move is to hold back.

We often celebrate bold, decisive action, yet history—military and otherwise—holds countless examples where success grew from calculated delay and controlled ambiguity. Operation Fortitude in 1944 remains a model of strategic misdirection. The Allies conjured entire phantom divisions, complete with fake radio chatter and planted intelligence, convincing German command that the D-Day landings would strike Pas de Calais instead of Normandy. The lesson here transcends warfare: power lies not only in what you do, but in how you shape what others believe you are about to do. In politics, negotiations, or corporate strategy, anticipating the interpretations and misinterpretations of your actions becomes a quiet but formidable advantage.

And this leads to a hard truth: decision-making under pressure rarely offers the luxury of full information. The 1976 Israeli raid on Entebbe Airport was planned and executed in under a week, with patchy intelligence and staggering risks. The mission's success hinged not on certainty but on building the best possible probabilities in an impossibly short time. Civilian leaders—whether CEOs confronting sudden market collapse, doctors making urgent medical calls, or parents guiding teenagers through crisis—face the same wager: act too soon and you may blunder; wait too long and you may lose everything. The finest leaders are not those who eliminate uncertainty, but those who can inhabit it long enough to act with conviction.

Yet strategy is not merely cerebral—it is moral. History makes this clear. The most infamous wartime atrocities—My Lai, Abu Ghraib, and countless others—did not stem from poor tactics but from ethical collapse. In the haze of war, cruelty can be rationalised as expedience, vengeance, or necessity. The civilian world is no cleaner: corporations slash safety for profit, politicians weaponise fear, institutions cause harm while calling it "policy." The discipline to maintain ethical clarity when conditions are murky is not a philosophical luxury—it is a hard-earned skill, often the one dividing the admirable from the merely competent.

Among the more neglected wartime disciplines is strategic empathy. Military history is too often told as a clash of forces, but beneath each clash lies a contest of perceptions. Skilled strategists do not just survey the terrain; they map the enemy's mind. What do they fear? Desire? Assume? This is not moral compromise—it is intelligence gathering of the most human kind. In civilian life, the same faculty proves indispensable. Whether diffusing workplace conflict, bridging cultural divides, or steering tense personal relationships, the ability to think beyond one's own vantage point can amplify influence and defuse confrontation. Empathy, wielded strategically, is anything but soft.

None of this is an argument for the nobility of war. The point is that certain human faculties—sharpened under its unforgiving conditions—can be reclaimed and put to work for peace. Imagine the rigour of a war room applied to climate negotiations; the discipline of a soldier channelled into emotional steadiness; the flexibility of an insurgent strategist turned towards social reform. These are not idle thought experiments. They are urgent questions in a world whose crises, from ecological collapse to political instability, grow sharper by the day.

It is worth remembering that some of the most enduring principles in military doctrine are aimed at avoiding conflict altogether. Sun Tzu again: "The supreme art of war is to subdue the enemy without fighting." Such wisdom travels easily into civilian life. De-escalation, diplomacy, and judicious compromise are not signs of timidity but of strategic maturity. We must shed the false divide between battlefield and boardroom, between warfare and wisdom. Tools honed in conflict, if reoriented, can strengthen not only our institutions but our individual character.

This is no romantic gloss over suffering, nor a casual mining of trauma for metaphors. It is a proposition—perhaps a radical one—that within the wreckage of past conflicts lies a storehouse of intelligence that, if understood rightly, can serve life rather than diminish it. Four domains—timing, decision-making, moral clarity, and empathy—stand out as especially ripe for translation into everyday practice. These are not lofty ideals; they are working instruments for thinking more lucidly, acting with greater purpose, and leading with integrity under pressure.

Whether you are an educator, entrepreneur, activist, executive, parent, or policymaker, what follows is not simply an account of what war has shown us. It is an argument for living more strategically—without waiting for disaster to force the lesson. For the soul, too, has its battlefield. Strategy belongs there as much as anywhere.

The Art of Timing and Patience:

To act at the wrong time is often worse than not acting at all. This is a principle that transcends warfare, threading its way through business negotiations, social movements, personal decisions, and diplomacy. It is one of the least glamorous disciplines of power and one of the most consequential. The art of timing—knowing when to act, when to wait, and when to appear inactive—requires a fusion of discipline, intuition, and foresight that few master and even fewer recognise as mastery. In warfare, as in life, patience is not a passive state but an active, strategic posture: a readiness held in restraint. As Sun Tzu warned over two millennia ago, "He who is prudent and lies in wait for an enemy who is not, will be victorious." The same prudence applies to those navigating the unpredictability of modern institutions, markets, and crises.

Timing is not merely about choosing the optimal moment. It is about shaping the moment. In this respect, the Cold War offers one of the richest archives of how nations weaponised waiting. The Cuban Missile Crisis of 1962 is often remembered for its brinkmanship—two superpowers teetering on the edge of nuclear war. But behind the drama was a series of exquisitely timed choices: carefully delayed communiqués, paused military actions, and backchannel diplomacy that unfolded hour by hour. What might look like hesitation was, in fact, a form of control. President Kennedy's decision to resist the temptation of immediate military retaliation in favour of a naval quarantine was a strategic act of temporal calibration. It allowed both sides to preserve dignity and recalibrate their options. The delay was not weakness. It was what kept the world from burning.

The strategic value of patience also emerges sharply in guerrilla warfare, where time becomes the weapon of the underdog. From the protracted resistance in Vietnam to the insurgencies in Afghanistan, irregular forces have often lacked firepower but compensated with temporal advantage. They understand that delay erodes morale, exhausts supply chains, and distorts perception. For them, survival is itself a form of pressure. The goal is not to win decisively but to ensure that the opponent cannot sustain engagement indefinitely. In this way, guerrilla strategy flips the logic of speed. Victory is not a function of rapid dominance, but of slow endurance. This is not unlike activist movements, social reform campaigns, or market disruption efforts in the civilian world, where success hinges less on sudden breakthroughs than on the sustained, quiet erosion of outdated paradigms.

What all of these scenarios share is a cultivated *tolerance for ambiguity.* The most dangerous leader—whether in politics, business, or war—is often the one who cannot sit with uncertainty, who acts simply to escape the discomfort of waiting. Impulsive action, dressed up as decisiveness, has sunk empires and companies alike. The 2003 Iraq invasion, premised on flawed intelligence and executed with insufficient patience for diplomatic or regional dynamics, is a stark reminder of what happens when readiness is confused with restlessness. Strategic patience is not paralysis. It is the ability to absorb tension without discharging it prematurely. And it often comes with psychological cost. It demands that one act with full force precisely when the moment permits—not before.

This raises a deeper insight: *timing is not the same as speed.* In the age of digital acceleration, where decisions are often made in minutes and leaders are evaluated by their responsiveness, the virtue of delay has become countercultural. But history suggests that some of the most effective decisions are slow-cooked. The Allied invasion of

Normandy in 1944 took over two years to plan. Success hinged not only on logistics but on *patience*—waiting for the right alignment of weather, intelligence, and enemy vulnerability. Had they acted earlier, without such careful calibration, the campaign might have collapsed. There is a difference between being fast and being right.

Equally important is the role of *intuition* in timing. Contrary to popular belief, the most experienced strategists do not rely on formulae alone. They blend analysis with instinct—a cultivated sensitivity to the rhythms of conflict, the psychology of the opponent, and the latent variables in play. In this, timing becomes an *art* as much as a science. It is not simply about data or precedent, but about perceiving the subtle inflection point where delay tips into opportunity. As military strategist Basil Liddell Hart once noted, "The most dangerous moment comes with victory." The implication is clear: even success must be timed correctly, lest it collapse under its own momentum.

This intuition is visible not only in military history, but in crisis leadership across disciplines. Consider how effective emergency response leaders prioritise their actions. In the aftermath of a disaster, whether natural or political, rushing in can cause more harm than good. Seasoned leaders understand when to stabilise, when to delegate, when to communicate, and when to act. Misjudging the sequence or tempo can undermine the entire effort. The art of timing, in such cases, becomes a matter of moral as well as operational significance.

Strategic patience is also inherently *relational*. It involves more than waiting on events—it often means waiting on people. Whether in conflict resolution, diplomacy, or even personal negotiation, acting prematurely can alienate the very stakeholders whose consent or trust is essential. The 1990s Good Friday Agreement in Northern Ireland took years of waiting, talking, and reframing entrenched narratives. Its architects understood that timing was not only about external conditions, but about internal readiness—when communities were tired enough of conflict, when leaders could risk appearing conciliatory, when compromise would not be mistaken for capitulation. The agreement did not happen when the conditions were ideal. It happened when *the perception of cost and gain shifted enough to permit a new future.*

What emerges across these examples is a central theme: *patience is not weakness, but strength under control.* It requires the ability to hold readiness in suspension. And this ability is transferable. In professional life, it applies to how leaders pace reform. In creative life, it relates to when and how ideas are released or developed. In personal life, it speaks to how we handle provocation, grief, ambition, or relational tension. We are not taught to wait well. Yet the most strategic minds understand that waiting, done well, is not passive—it is power deferred until the moment when its impact is maximised.

That moment, of course, does not announce itself. This is what makes the art of timing so elusive. There are no guarantees. But there are disciplines. One can learn to monitor not just events, but emotional conditions, stakeholder dynamics, and psychological thresholds. One can learn to tell the difference between fear-based delay and wisdom-based restraint. And one can learn to ask the right questions: *Is this the moment to act—or the moment to prepare? Am I driven by clarity or discomfort? Will this move strengthen my position—or merely satisfy my ego?*

Sun Tzu's insistence that one should know both the enemy and oneself has a temporal dimension. Timing demands self-knowledge: the ability to discern when one's own impulses, insecurities, or ego are distorting perception. It also demands knowledge of context—what is shifting beneath the surface, what is being missed in the noise, and what future conditions may arise if one holds steady. The best tacticians are not reactive. They are temporally literate. They know how to live in the interval between stimulus and response—and make that interval their domain.

The art of timing is not about passively waiting for the right conditions. It is about *shaping one's readiness* so that, when the moment comes, one is not merely present, but prepared. This is not a mindset that comes naturally. It must be cultivated. It requires rejecting the cult of immediacy, tolerating the discomfort of ambiguity, and embracing the discipline of strategic restraint. Whether in matters of war or in the conduct of one's private or professional life, those who learn to wait well gain an edge not through control of others, but through control of themselves. And that, ultimately, is the most decisive form of power.

Decision Under Duress:

Crises do not create leaders. They reveal them. When time is short, options are murky, and consequences irreversible, decision-making under duress becomes not merely a tactical exercise but a test of character, perception, and nerve. The ability to think clearly amid chaos is not the absence of emotion—it is the discipline of ordering emotion toward judgement. And while peacetime decision-making often permits reflection, revision, and feedback, high-stakes decisions, especially in war or extreme environments, force an entirely different mental model: one where ambiguity must be navigated without paralysis, and boldness must coexist with precision.

The Israeli Entebbe raid of 1976 remains a defining case study in this high-pressure calculus. Following the hijacking of an Air France plane by pro-Palestinian and German terrorists and its diversion to Uganda, Israeli authorities were presented with an impossible decision matrix: allow hostages to be executed, attempt a negotiation with a brutal regime, or orchestrate a military operation 2,500 miles from home with minimal intelligence and no guarantee of success. What unfolded was Operation Thunderbolt—a surprise commando raid that rescued 102 hostages in under 90 minutes, eliminating the terrorists and sustaining minimal Israeli casualties. But behind the operation's legendary execution lay a week of fevered decision-making that balanced military daring with moral restraint.

What makes Entebbe such a compelling model is not only its operational brilliance but its *cognitive choreography*. Decision-makers had to evaluate political implications, logistical feasibility, host-nation hostility, and human risk in compressed time. Success demanded *constraint-based creativity*: working within extreme limits to discover non-obvious options. The choice was not between action and inaction but among several equally dangerous courses. This mirrors dilemmas often faced in executive leadership or crisis governance—where information is partial, costs are unpredictable, and the status quo is collapsing. At such moments, the worst sin is not error but inertia.

The Allied deception campaign preceding D-Day in 1944—Operation Bodyguard—offers a contrasting but equally instructive model. Rather than operate within minutes or days, planners took months to design and sustain an elaborate fiction: that the invasion of Europe would occur at Pas de Calais, not Normandy. This required not just feints and dummy equipment, but the manipulation of German pattern-recognition: creating false radio traffic, deploying double agents, and carefully leaking misinformation to simulate authenticity. This was a decision made not under fire but under fog—the fog of a future battlefield yet to be shaped. The brilliance of the operation was its patience. High-stakes decisions are not always about acting fast. Sometimes they are about *engineering perception* over time so that the opponent chooses wrongly. Strategic leadership, in this view, is not reactive but generative.

Both cases reveal that decision under duress is not a single act—it is a choreography of choices across actors, levels, and moments. It requires a central question: *What is the real risk we are managing?* In Entebbe, it was the risk of hostage death versus the risk of international escalation. In D-Day deception, it was the risk of catastrophic amphibious failure versus the risk of being discovered in the act of manipulation. Understanding this deeper frame clarifies not only the objective but the logic of sacrifice. High-stakes decisions almost always involve trade-offs. But the best decisions identify *which variables are negotiable* and which are not. That clarity is not always obvious in the moment. It must be imposed.

This is why leadership in crisis requires more than intelligence. It demands *decision readiness*: a state of cognitive and moral preparedness to absorb complexity without simplification. The most effective crisis leaders rehearse scenarios—not to script the future, but to prime their minds for layered thinking under pressure. The Israeli planners of Entebbe didn't invent their strategy from scratch. They drew from rehearsed doctrines, historical analogues, and a culture of improvisation honed under existential threat. Readiness is not prediction. It is *friction-tested adaptability*. In this sense, the military principle of "train as you fight" holds broader wisdom. Leaders who prepare only for ideal conditions will fracture under real ones.

Modern entrepreneurship increasingly echoes this wartime reality. Tech founders navigating financial crashes, CEOs steering through public scandals, and activists coordinating mass mobilisation amid repression all confront decisions that echo battlefield complexity. The compressed timeline of high-growth industries often creates dilemmas where no choice is clearly right, and all have reputational or structural risk. Leaders who survive such environments exhibit not genius but *disciplined improvisation.* They know when to pivot, when to escalate, when to wait, and when to signal decisiveness even before full clarity has arrived.

But decision under duress also brings a darker temptation: to displace accountability in the name of urgency. The pressure to act can become a shield for poor thinking or moral shortcuts. History is replete with decisions made in haste that resulted in prolonged catastrophe—from the 1914 mobilisation orders that led to World War I, to the 2008 financial bailouts structured without adequate long-term safeguards. The lesson is not that speed is the enemy, but that *urgency must be matched with rigour.* A good decision under pressure is not necessarily the fastest—it is the one that can withstand the weight of its consequences.

This calls for a refined decision architecture. When operating under pressure, effective leaders often break problems into constrained modules: what is reversible and what is not? What must be decided now, and what can wait? Who has the clearest insight into each domain? The Entebbe raid succeeded because it was not overly centralised. Tactical command rested with those nearest to the action. Strategic guidance came from the top. This delegation by logic, not hierarchy, enabled speed *and* accuracy. In civilian crises—whether organisational, familial, or civic—this modular approach allows teams to act rapidly while minimising blind spots. The key is not omniscience, but *structured decentralisation.*

Another critical insight is the role of *psychological poise.* Decision under duress tests not only intellect but temperament. Fear distorts time perception. Adrenaline warps consequence estimation. Leaders who mistake pressure for clarity often over-commit to the first plausible path. But those with emotional fluency learn to metabolise stress without outsourcing it to the group. This is a leadership skill rarely taught but constantly tested. The world does not need fewer emotional leaders. It needs more emotionally *disciplined* ones—those who can absorb collective anxiety, metabolise it, and reframe it into strategic clarity.

At the heart of decision under duress lies a paradox: *you must act decisively while knowing you might be wrong*. This calls not for arrogance, but for a cultivated humility—a willingness to act without omniscience, to revise mid-course, and to own outcomes without deflecting. Some of history's greatest decisions were not those made with full confidence, but those made with *deliberate uncertainty*. Eisenhower's D-Day letter, prepared in case of failure, accepted personal blame in advance. That kind of integrity allows teams to commit fully. Trust is the invisible currency of rapid execution.

Decision-making frameworks under pressure must therefore include moral scaffolding. Not because every situation offers a clean ethical path, but because *ethical clarity enhances functional clarity*. When the team knows what lines will not be crossed, they can innovate boldly within those bounds. This clarity is stabilising. It allows speed without recklessness, risk without cynicism. The absence of such clarity often results in decisions that win battles but lose legitimacy—whether in the courtroom, the boardroom, or the public square.

Finally, the most transferable insight from high-stakes wartime decision-making is this: *crisis does not change who we are; it reveals who we have trained ourselves to become*. Under duress, our defaults surface. Leaders who have cultivated self-awareness, prepared their teams for ambiguity, and rehearsed their values under low-stakes conditions are those best equipped to lead when the margins narrow. The rest, however brilliant in theory, will find themselves overwhelmed by velocity, complexity, and fear.

To decide well under pressure is not a gift. It is a discipline—earned through exposure, reflection, failure, and the hard work of building inner architecture long before it is tested. Those who master it do not merely survive crisis. They shape it. And in doing so, they model a kind of leadership that transcends war: the ability to act wisely when wisdom seems least available.

"Moral Clarity in Foggy Conditions":

Part 1

No decision made in a combat zone is ever clean. Orders are given in partial light, threats evolve by the minute, and consequences stretch far beyond the moment of execution. And yet, within this chaos, soldiers are often expected to act with precision not only tactically, but morally. The same expectation increasingly extends to civilians navigating corporate malfeasance, institutional failure, or rapidly shifting ethical terrain. The modern professional may not wear a uniform or carry a weapon, but the dilemmas they face—when truth is contested, harm is distributed, and values collide—can be just as morally charged. The question is not whether we know right from wrong in theory. The question is whether we can *see* clearly enough to act rightly when the field is obscured by ambiguity.

In war, this ambiguity has a name: the fog of war. Coined by the 19th-century military strategist Carl von Clausewitz, it refers not only to physical disorientation but to *informational distortion*. Troop movements misreported, intentions misread, consequences miscalculated. But the fog is not only tactical. It is *moral*. One of the most disorienting features of modern conflict is that it often resists a clean division between villain and victim. Consider the use of human shields by combatants, the targeting of dual-use infrastructure like power stations, or the deployment of drones in civilian-populated areas. Here, legal frameworks may be technically satisfied, yet ethical clarity dissolves.

The My Lai Massacre during the Vietnam War remains one of the most painful illustrations of moral collapse under pressure. American soldiers, believing they were under threat from Viet Cong operatives, executed hundreds of unarmed civilians, including women and children. The justifications given—fog of war, confusion, operational stress—did not obscure the atrocity. Yet they pointed to something deeper: *the psychological ease with which moral standards degrade when context is unstable and peer pressure is strong.* This pattern is not confined to war zones. It replays itself in corporate boardrooms, political campaigns, hospital triage protocols, and even algorithmic design meetings—anywhere decisions are rushed, accountability is diffused, and values are subordinated to urgency.

To maintain ethical integrity under such conditions requires more than rules. It requires *moral orientation.* Just as navigators in a storm use fixed stars to chart direction, leaders in ambiguity need internal compasses—principles that remain stable even as circumstances shift. But to function, those principles must be more than slogans. They must be *practised*, interrogated, and stress-tested in advance. One of the most common errors in ethical breakdowns is not malevolence, but *unreadiness.* People default to tribal loyalty, institutional inertia, or reactive justifications because they have not built the cognitive musculature for complexity.

The philosopher Michael Walzer, in his seminal work *Just and Unjust Wars*, insists that soldiers do not escape moral judgement simply because they are "following orders." Nor can citizens claim neutrality in systems they benefit from but do not question. Ethical agency, he argues, must be exercised precisely when it is most difficult—when risk is high, clarity is low, and precedent is unclear. What Walzer captures is a critical truth: *moral fog does not relieve us of responsibility; it amplifies the need for discernment.* This is why simplistic codes or binary doctrines so often fail. What's needed instead is ethical literacy—an ability to hold conflicting values in tension without collapsing into paralysis.

This literacy involves asking layered questions: What do I know, and how reliable is that knowledge? What risks am I managing—and to whom? What values are at stake, and are they mine or merely inherited? Is my reaction grounded in principle or panic? These questions are not luxuries; they are safeguards. In the Israeli Defence Forces, the practice of *Tohar HaNeshek*—"purity of arms"—seeks to instil this layered thinking. It teaches that the power to act violently must be constrained by an equally strong commitment to human dignity. Soldiers are trained not merely to follow orders, but to assess whether those orders meet a higher ethical test. The expectation is not perfection—but *moral alertness under duress.*

This approach translates powerfully into civilian life. Consider whistleblowers in large institutions—those who resist complicit silence at personal cost. Edward Snowden's disclosures about mass surveillance, or Frances Haugen's release of Facebook's internal documents, were acts not of disloyalty but of *ethical insurgency*—a willingness to pierce institutional fog in order to restore moral visibility. Whether one agrees with their methods or not, such cases ask us to confront a disturbing reality: that systems often reward conformity over clarity, and that moral action may require *institutional disobedience*.

But moral clarity does not mean moral certainty. The danger of overcompensating for fog is becoming dogmatic—mistaking one's perspective for universal truth. This is where humility becomes not a weakness, but a *disciplinary tool*. The most reliable moral actors are often those who approach their decisions with a kind of *confident humility*—knowing what they stand for, but willing to revise in light of new evidence or deeper reflection. The Geneva Conventions were not designed by saints but by realists who understood that even in war, restraint is possible. Their power lies not in perfection, but in *bounded aspiration*: drawing lines so that human dignity is not completely eclipsed by necessity.

In complex environments, the search for ethical action is rarely about locating a perfect answer. It is about identifying *a justifiable one*—a decision that, though imperfect, can be defended with coherence, context, and conscience. And that means constructing a moral audit trail. Military leaders who document their deliberations—even privately—help future generations learn from moral mistakes. The same holds true in medicine, law, engineering, and journalism. A robust ethical process must be *transparent enough to critique, resilient enough to withstand scrutiny*, and adaptive enough to evolve with complexity.

Historical episodes like the Allied bombing of Dresden or the U.S. use of atomic weapons in Japan underscore how even victorious powers are not absolved of moral reckoning. Retrospective clarity does not always translate to contemporaneous wisdom. Yet it is precisely the pain of hindsight that should drive better foresight. If leaders are to avoid becoming agents of rationalised harm, they must develop the habit of ethical rehearsal: imagining not only what action is expedient, but what narrative will be written in its aftermath.

Moral clarity in foggy conditions is not the product of genius. It is the product of discipline. Discipline in seeking context before action. Discipline in resisting false binaries. Discipline in holding power accountable—not as a punishment, but as a principle of stewardship. War may dramatise these choices, but they are embedded in everyday life: in how teachers handle bias, how doctors navigate triage, how voters assess trade-offs. The battlefield only makes visible what is always latent: *that integrity is not the absence of conflict, but the presence of discernment in conflict.*

(Part 2 – Continuation of "Moral Clarity in Foggy Conditions")

To navigate moral complexity in a durable way requires what theologian Dietrich Bonhoeffer once described as "responsible realism"—a posture that neither retreats into idealism nor collapses into cynicism. Bonhoeffer, writing and acting against Nazism from within Germany, understood better than most that ethical clarity must operate under conditions of danger, compromise, and incomplete knowledge. He advocated for a form of moral courage grounded in *situational awareness* rather than abstraction: the ability to understand who is harmed, what systems are being preserved, and whether one's actions serve human dignity or merely institutional momentum.

This concept carries potent relevance for leadership in today's fragmented information ecosystems. A modern CEO responding to AI ethics concerns, a civil servant managing asylum policy, or a team lead navigating internal discrimination allegations may each be forced to decide amidst incomplete data, competing loyalties, and conflicting definitions of fairness. Moral clarity, in these cases, is not about bold declarations. It is about *measured integrity*—the ability to act while leaving space for self-interrogation. Where the moral landscape is fractured, a single clear step forward may be more valuable than a grand ethical posture. Precision matters more than purity.

Part of what makes this clarity difficult is our innate tendency to rationalise harm. Cognitive dissonance theory shows how we adjust our beliefs to accommodate our actions, particularly under stress. A soldier may convince himself that a civilian posed a threat to justify a lethal mistake; a policymaker may dehumanise migrants to preserve a draconian border policy. This psychological dynamic reveals an uncomfortable truth: *the fog is often internal before it is external.* We obscure from ourselves the harm we cause by narrating it in noble terms. The antidote is not guilt, but reflection—systems of accountability that bring us back into contact with those affected by our decisions.

This is why ethical clarity also requires *proximity*. Philosopher Martha Nussbaum argues that moral judgement is sharpened not by abstract rule-making but by *narrative engagement*—listening to the stories of those most impacted. In post-conflict reconciliation efforts, such as South Africa's Truth and Reconciliation Commission or Rwanda's Gacaca courts, victims' testimonies were not only therapeutic; they were epistemological. They made the abstract harms of policy or ideology *visceral.* The takeaway for contemporary ethical leadership is this: *if you cannot hear the voices of those at the margins of your decision, your moral compass is incomplete.*

But clarity is not merely empathetic—it is strategic. In military terms, ethical restraint can enhance legitimacy, build local alliances, and reduce insurgency. In business, it preserves trust and pre-empts reputational collapse. In governance, it strengthens rule of law and civic confidence. These are not secondary benefits. They are *core outcomes* of morally attuned leadership. When leaders mistake ambiguity for licence, or treat fog as camouflage, they may win the moment but lose the long game. True resilience—whether national or organisational—is built not on expedience, but on values that can endure scrutiny.

To operationalise moral clarity, leaders must develop three habits: *ethical anticipation*, *structured deliberation*, and *public accountability*. Ethical anticipation means scanning ahead for dilemmas before they harden into crisis—much like a commander reading terrain for ambush potential. Structured deliberation ensures that decisions are not rushed through charisma or urgency, but subjected to multiple lenses—legal, psychological, social. And public accountability means crafting decisions that one would be willing to explain not only to a boardroom, but to history itself. This is not idealism. It is *defensive design*: protecting institutions and individuals from corrosive short-termism.

Examples abound of what this looks like in practice. When New Zealand Prime Minister Jacinda Ardern faced the Christchurch terrorist attacks, her rapid yet empathetic response—visiting families, tightening gun laws, and refusing to name the perpetrator—was not improvised but rooted in coherent ethical leadership. Her clarity did not come from knowing every answer, but from knowing *what not to compromise*. Likewise, when former U.S. military lawyer Alberto Mora challenged the Pentagon's use of torture during the early 2000s, he did so not because it was politically convenient but because it violated the constitutional and moral foundations of the service he had pledged to uphold. Their decisions were not reactive. They were *prepared*.

This preparation is the final lesson. The best time to cultivate moral clarity is not when fog descends, but when skies are clear. Institutions that rehearse ethical decision-making under low-stakes conditions are more likely to respond coherently under stress. Scenario planning, red-teaming ethical risks, embedding dissent into decision loops—these are not luxuries. They are *infrastructures of integrity*. And when they are absent, we see the same failures recur: complicity masked as loyalty, legality mistaken for legitimacy, and silence mistaken for wisdom.

Moral clarity is not a beam of divine light. It is the result of human effort—repeated, refined, and rooted in conviction. It does not require perfection, but it demands *awareness*. And awareness, once cultivated, becomes a kind of armour: not to shield against criticism, but to ensure that when the fog settles, you can still see yourself clearly. The battlefield may be literal or metaphorical. The choices may be grand or granular. But the principle is universal: *even when you cannot see the whole field, you can still act with honour*.

And that, in the final analysis, is the truest test of leadership—not how one acts when the way is clear, but how one chooses when it is not.

Strategic Empathy: Thinking Like the Adversary to Transcend the Conflict

The most underestimated skill in conflict—whether in war, business, politics, or personal relationships—is the ability to think not *about* one's adversary, but *like* them. Strategic empathy is not an act of moral surrender, but a form of cognitive strength. It demands the discipline to step beyond one's assumptions and enter the logic of another's position, not to imitate or endorse it, but to illuminate it. Where most responses to opposition begin with resistance or judgment, strategic empathy begins with curiosity. What does this person value? What are they protecting? What fears animate their posture? These are not sentimental questions. They are strategic ones.

The military strategist Sun Tzu captured this thousands of years ago with unsettling clarity: *"If you know the enemy and know yourself, you need not fear the result of a hundred battles."* Crucially, this was not about moral alignment but cognitive proximity. To know the enemy is not merely to surveil their capabilities, but to understand the mental models that shape their choices. Yet even today, this advice is frequently misunderstood or under-applied. Instead of seeking to grasp the opponent's perspective, we caricature it—reducing them to motives we find more comfortable to loathe than to understand.

A compelling example comes from the Cold War, when the failure to practice strategic empathy nearly plunged the world into nuclear annihilation. During the 1962 Cuban Missile Crisis, American military officials initially interpreted Soviet actions as pure aggression. But it was only when President John F. Kennedy and his advisors began considering Nikita Khrushchev's *internal pressures*—domestic insecurity, perception of Western encirclement, and need to maintain prestige among allies—that de-escalatory backchannels emerged. The insight wasn't that Khrushchev was right, but that he was *rational within his own frame*. Understanding that frame allowed Kennedy to craft a resolution that preserved dignity on both sides—

a naval blockade instead of an airstrike, and a secret quid pro quo involving U.S. missiles in Turkey.

This principle is equally vital beyond geopolitics. In negotiation strategy, the work of Harvard's Roger Fisher and William Ury on "getting to yes" popularised the idea that positional bargaining is far less effective than *interest-based negotiation.* That is, instead of fixating on *what* the other party demands, seek to understand *why* they demand it. When negotiators shift from defending turf to uncovering underlying needs—security, recognition, fairness—they uncover solutions that may satisfy both sides. Strategic empathy becomes not a concession, but an *unlock.*

In corporate leadership, the absence of strategic empathy often leads to costly missteps. Consider the infamous case of New Coke. In 1985, Coca-Cola reformulated its flagship product in response to taste tests and market data—assuming consumers would logically prefer a better-tasting drink. What they failed to consider was the *emotional and symbolic attachment* millions of Americans had to the original Coke as a cultural icon. The backlash was swift and unforgiving. The company had excellent market intelligence but no empathy map. They knew what people liked on paper. They did not grasp what people *believed.*

Strategic empathy is particularly challenging when we feel morally superior to the other party. The temptation is to dehumanise, flatten, or explain away their position as ignorance or malice. But to lead effectively—whether in peace negotiations, policy debates, or organisational conflict—requires resisting that temptation. Former U.S. President Barack Obama, during the healthcare reform debates, often noted that "you have to give the other side a way to say yes." This requires recognising not only *your* goals, but *their* constraints. What are they afraid of losing? What constituencies do they answer to? What narrative will allow them to reverse course without humiliation? These are the practical ingredients of sustainable compromise.

Empathy here does not mean agreement. It means clarity. It means that before we respond to others, we take the time to consider how *they* would explain themselves—not to justify, but to navigate. In psychological terms, this is known as *theory of mind*: the ability to model the internal states of others. It is not just a social virtue but a cognitive tool. Studies have shown that people with high theory-of-mind abilities make better decisions in dynamic environments—because they can anticipate not just *what* others will do, but *why*.

Even in the most brutal environments—like interrogation, insurgency warfare, or hostage negotiation—strategic empathy can be the difference between escalation and resolution. The FBI's crisis negotiation unit, for example, trains agents not in threats or force, but in *active listening*. They teach that rapport precedes compliance. Understanding the emotional logic of the hostage-taker is not weakness—it is the most efficient path to de-escalation. To treat empathy as "soft" is to confuse sensitivity with sophistication.

This distinction becomes even more critical in polarised societies, where ideological opponents often exist in epistemic silos. If people derive their moral and factual beliefs from different information ecosystems, then persuasion requires not only evidence but *framing*. As behavioural economist Dan Ariely notes, people are more likely to shift positions when they feel *heard* first. Strategic empathy, then, becomes a precondition for influence. It says: before you argue, listen deeply enough to model their fears, their pride, their pain.

What makes this so difficult is that it demands temporary self-suspension. To think like one's opponent is to set aside—if only for a moment—your own moral certainties. That can feel disloyal to your cause or to yourself. But this is where strategic empathy differs from moral relativism. It is not the abandonment of judgement, but the postponement of it for the sake of precision. You cannot effectively counter what you do not truly understand. *Precision, not pity, is the currency of strategic empathy.*

One might ask: what about truly immoral opponents? Should one seek to empathise with extremists, warmongers, or abusers? The answer is: only if your goal is to change behaviour or prevent harm. Moral outrage may fuel protest or catharsis. But effective action often requires *comprehension before condemnation*. For example, former extremists who now lead de-radicalisation programmes consistently report that it was *being understood*—not shamed—that began their exit from toxic ideologies. Strategic empathy, even with those who appear monstrous, can be a way of interrupting harm at its root.

In professional environments, strategic empathy scales down in equally powerful ways. A manager handling a resistant team member, a startup co-founder facing investor pushback, a teacher confronting student defiance—all face versions of adversarial energy. The choice is often between escalation and exploration. Strategic empathy asks: what would I believe if I were in their shoes? What are they protecting? What do they feel they must signal, and to whom? Such questions change the tone of the interaction. They open doors.

Ultimately, strategic empathy is not only about others. It is a diagnostic lens for the self. When we practise it rigorously, we begin to recognise our own blind spots, our own echo chambers, our own defensive routines. To imagine how we look from the outside is to disrupt the autopilot of our own identity. This is why strategic empathy is a discipline—it requires effort, imagination, and the humility to be changed by what one sees.

To train oneself in this is to cultivate an uncommon advantage. Not simply to outmanoeuvre, but to out-understand. To disarm hostility by decoding it. To unlock cooperation by seeing what lies beneath resistance. Strategic empathy is not about surrendering your position. It is about *seeing the full chessboard.* And in a world driven increasingly by misrecognition, there may be no more vital skill.

Chapter 9
War Without Guns: Psychological, Economic, and Cultural Battlefields

War has never truly been bound by trenches, borders, or stockpiles of weapons. It has always seeped into the mind, the marketplace, and the gallery just as readily as it stains the battlefield. The twentieth century—punctuated by global conflagrations and the arrival of the televised casualty count—trained the public to picture conflict in its most kinetic form: bombs tumbling from the sky, soldiers advancing, nations falling. But that image, however enduring, is now misleading. In our own century, the battlefield has diffused into unseen arenas—data streams, banking systems, cultural narratives, and even the unspoken recesses of the human mind. The era we call "peace" might be more honestly labelled "non-violent war," where the weapons are subtle, the territory psychological, and the wounds no less real.

The front line has shifted inward. It cuts through newsfeeds, through the words we use, through the contours of identity. You see it in the packaging of truth, in the political recasting of history, in the quiet fraying of cultural fabric. This is war fought not with shells and shrapnel, but with meaning itself. Here, we will explore how the idea of warfare has expanded beyond traditional battlefields—and why this expansion calls for new habits of vigilance, literacy, and self-possession.

Few changes illustrate this better than the elevation of narrative into a weapon. For ancient empires, legitimacy could rest on bloodlines, monuments, or divine sanction. Today, it is constructed in perception—by whoever seizes the microphone first, shouts the loudest, or crafts the most convincing fiction. The Cold War ended without a direct missile exchange, yet it was hardly without ammunition: radio broadcasts, pamphlets, cinema, doctrine—all poured into the civilian sphere. The Soviet Union, in particular, invested heavily in disinformation, planting calculated falsehoods in Western discourse to erode trust, deepen divisions, and deflect blame. What was then the preserve of state apparatus is now commonplace, thanks to the democratising effect of digital media. Modern psychological operations—spread through memes, bot networks, and algorithm-driven echo chambers—no longer depend on credibility or internal consistency. Their aim is not to persuade so much as to disorient, to corrode the very possibility of certainty. The objective is not belief—it is the slow attrition of belief itself.

This is not the stuff of abstract theory. Russian interference in the 2016 US election, the shaping of public sentiment through TikTok or X (formerly Twitter), the exploitation of Facebook in Myanmar to incite violence against the Rohingya—each is an example of the narrative as an operational theatre. In China, entire cultural communities have been recast as existential threats to national unity, their internment justified as counter-extremism. These are not side effects of war; they are its main campaign. Win the narrative and you build the moral scaffolding upon which all actions are judged.

But narrative is only one prong of soft power. Economics—long treated as a separate domain—has become an active tool of coercion. Sanctions, embargoes, trade restrictions now function as the sieges of the globalised age. Take Iran: under the weight of sanctions, its economy withered, medicine ran scarce, inflation ballooned—yet few bombs fell. Or Russia: following the invasion of Ukraine, its access to global financial systems was choked off, assets frozen, oligarchs targeted, sectors disrupted—all without a single warhead. Such measures are not neutral levers; they are calibrated to trigger internal strain, to weaponise scarcity, to push societies towards concessions under duress.

Nor is economic warfare always aimed abroad. At home, austerity programmes, structural adjustments, and capital flight can be wielded with a surgeon's detachment from the social havoc they produce. In Greece, Argentina, and elsewhere, whole generations have been marked by fiscal measures dictated from afar—policies presented as prudent economics but experienced as humiliation, dependency, and loss of sovereignty. These conflicts wear no uniforms, but their casualties are counted all the same.

Then there is cultural warfare—subtler, perhaps, but no less destructive. Erasing a people need not mean erasing their bodies. It can mean dismantling their rituals, distorting their history, or commandeering their symbols. When the Taliban obliterated the Bamiyan Buddhas in 2001, it was not only a gesture of religious extremism—it was a calculated strike against a shared cultural memory, a public declaration that one order had been extinguished and another enthroned. Colonial regimes, too, understood the tactic: in much of Africa and Southeast Asia, schooling was re-engineered to teach that local histories were primitive, languages backward, traditions obsolete. The extraction of resources was only part of the plunder; the rest was the quiet reprogramming of identity.

A civilisation's durability rests not solely on its infrastructure or treasury, but on what might be called its cultural immune system—its capacity to maintain narrative coherence, transmit memory across generations, and guard meaning from distortion. This has become more urgent in a globalised order that smooths distinctions, standardises behaviour, and often rewards imitation over originality. The danger is not a vibrant cosmopolitanism, but a thinning of the cultural blood—a drift towards sameness that makes manipulation easier.

And still, one battleground remains almost entirely overlooked: the one within. Each day, the modern individual faces an unrelenting drizzle of existential questions—Who am I? What matters? What is true?—delivered not in philosophical treatises but in push notifications, comparison feeds, and the quiet pull of advertising. Hyperconnectivity fractures identity, commodifies purpose, and normalises a low-grade hum of anxiety. It is a kind of constant psychic skirmish, an inner fog of war. Just as field commanders require clarity under fire, so too must civilians cultivate the ability to move through ambiguity without surrendering to cynicism or despair.

The tools of military survival—triage, prioritisation, chain of command, contingency planning—can have unexpected civilian applications. Veterans rebuilding their sense of self after the collapse of old certainties often discover methods for navigating chaos: disciplined thought, emotional steadiness, situational awareness. The extremity of war tends to strip away the inessential, forcing moral clarity. Choices sharpen. Values reveal themselves. Time compresses. Traumatic though it may be, that compression can also yield illumination.

To examine war without bullets is not to examine peace—it is to confront conflict in its most diffuse and enduring shapes. This is neither lament nor alarm bell, but an invitation: to widen our sense of what counts as aggression, to see through the spectacle of overt violence into the structures of manipulation beneath it, to reclaim agency in arenas too easily dismissed as non-combat zones. The aim is not to militarise our thinking, but to foster an alertness—a mental agility, as strategist John Boyd might put it—that allows us to respond with intelligence rather than react out of habit.

What follows will draw on case studies from Soviet-era disinformation to present-day algorithmic persuasion; on economic analyses that treat sanctions as both fiscal and psychological weaponry; on cultural accounts of indigenous resilience; and on introspective frameworks for recognising the conflicts embedded in daily life. This is not just a study of "them." It is a study of us—and the wars we inhabit, often without knowing it, every single day.

Narrative as Weapon

A war fought with words can devastate more permanently than one fought with weapons. Bullets tear flesh, but stories shape perception—and perception governs action. In the modern world, truth is not just contested but engineered. Narratives, once tools of meaning-making, have become instruments of strategic manipulation. The most effective weapons now are not missiles but memes, not soldiers but influencers, not invasions but insinuations. The frontline is cognitive, not geographic. *Storytelling is no longer ancillary to warfare; it is its vanguard.*

The strategic use of narrative has long been recognised by regimes seeking to consolidate power. The Soviet Union institutionalised disinformation as a tool of statecraft, not merely to obscure facts but to dismantle the very architecture of trust. During the Cold War, Soviet operatives didn't just deny the West's accusations—they flooded public discourse with so many alternative accounts that the notion of objective truth itself became suspect. For instance, Operation INFEKTION, a Soviet campaign in the 1980s, seeded the rumour that the CIA had invented HIV/AIDS. It was false, absurd even, yet it spread globally, appearing in newspapers, radio broadcasts, and student protests from Delhi to Dakar. The aim was never to convince with evidence but to destabilise through doubt. If everything might be a lie, then *nothing* is necessarily true.

The effectiveness of such campaigns stemmed from their ability to hijack the mechanisms of storytelling. Disinformation doesn't demand belief; it demands attention. It leverages repetition, emotional appeal, and cultural cues to short-circuit critical thinking. These are not flaws in the human psyche—they are features of it. People are not blank slates but narrative beings. They understand the world through plotlines, heroes and villains, beginnings and ends. When reality becomes too complex, they reach for stories. And the one who supplies the most accessible, compelling story, regardless of its accuracy, often wins.

This is not merely a Soviet relic. Today's information operations are decentralised, digitised, and disturbingly effective. In Myanmar, military officials used Facebook to incite genocidal hatred against the Rohingya minority, exploiting religious fault lines with coordinated fake accounts and fabricated atrocities. In the United States, Russian troll farms such as the Internet Research Agency stoked racial and political tensions during the 2016 election—not by fabricating votes, but by fabricating narratives. Their goal was not electoral victory per se but institutional erosion: to make democracy look dysfunctional, hypocritical, and hopeless.

The platform shift from pamphlet to pixel has intensified both the speed and scale of narrative warfare. Social media's architecture incentivises virality, not veracity. The most widely shared posts tend to be emotionally charged, simplistic, and polarising—precisely the attributes of effective propaganda. Algorithms, designed to maximise engagement, reward outrage and penalise nuance. They create epistemic silos where facts are optional and identity is reinforced through affirmation, not interrogation. *The battlefield is now your phone. The weapons are ideas that don't look like weapons at all.*

This transformation has blurred the line between state actor and civilian participant. Narrative war no longer belongs exclusively to governments. Anyone with a smartphone can shape perception, alter discourse, or spread distortion. In the case of the 2020 Delhi riots, incendiary WhatsApp forwards—often doctored or entirely fabricated—fanned flames of communal violence. Individuals became nodes in a decentralised information war, many unaware they were combatants. What makes modern narrative war so insidious is that it often appears as *conversation* rather than command, as *information* rather than intention.

But why does narrative wield such influence? It is not simply because stories are persuasive. It is because they confer coherence. In times of uncertainty, people gravitate toward narratives that provide moral clarity, causality, and closure. The danger is that the most comforting stories are often the most corrosive. They identify scapegoats. They simplify complexity. They transform systemic failure into individual betrayal. Consider the rise of conspiracy theories during the COVID-19 pandemic. In the absence of consistent messaging, people clung to explanatory narratives—however implausible—that made emotional sense. These narratives often included clear villains (governments, scientists, minorities), heroic resistors, and a hidden "truth" suppressed by elites. The parallels to war propaganda are unmistakable.

The implications for democratic societies are profound. In narrative warfare, the target is not just an election result or a public policy—it is the cognitive immunity of a population. Trust becomes a vulnerability. Institutions are reframed as enemies. Expertise is recast as elitism. The public sphere is turned into a theatre of perpetual doubt, where every claim requires suspicion and every rebuttal reinforces the conspiracy. This is not disagreement. It is a form of epistemological sabotage. And it has consequences for everything from vaccine uptake to climate response to interethnic peace.

What, then, are the defences against narrative warfare? The reflexive answer—fact-checking—misses the point. Facts alone do not dislodge stories. They must be embedded within *counter-narratives* that are equally resonant, equally human, and grounded in shared values.

The lesson from wartime propaganda is that people don't change their minds through information. They change when they *feel seen*, when the new story doesn't shame their previous belief but *integrates* it into a broader, more inclusive understanding.

Strategic communication, then, is not about shouting louder or censoring harder. It is about listening smarter. In contexts of polarisation, narratives must be designed not to dominate but to *connect*. During the conflict in Colombia, community radio stations played a vital role in peace-building—not by countering propaganda with fact sheets, but by amplifying local voices, lived experience, and common suffering. In Rwanda, post-genocide storytelling projects helped survivors and perpetrators narrate their trauma in ways that reclaimed dignity and resisted manipulation. These efforts were not naive. They were tactical. *Empathy can be a form of resistance.*

There is a parallel lesson for leadership in all domains—political, organisational, personal. Leaders today are not merely managers of operations. They are curators of narrative ecosystems. The stories they tell (and tolerate) shape the decision-making climate. A narrative of scarcity, for example, can justify unethical behaviour in business. A narrative of existential threat can rationalise authoritarian overreach. In each case, storytelling is not decoration—it is infrastructure. It sets the conditions for what becomes acceptable, thinkable, or even imaginable.

To navigate this terrain responsibly requires a dual literacy: narrative awareness and narrative discipline. Narrative awareness means recognising when you are being recruited into a plotline—when your emotions are being leveraged to serve someone else's frame. Narrative discipline means resisting the temptation to simplify, to scapegoat, or to engineer false certainty. It means learning to live with ambiguity without surrendering to paralysis.

Storytelling has always been a source of human power. But in the digital age, that power has been amplified, accelerated, and monetised. If narrative is now a weapon, then literacy is armour. Not just the ability to read, but the capacity to interpret, contextualise, and interrogate what is being presented as truth. The stakes are not theoretical. Wars are already being fought—without armies, without borders, and often without awareness. The challenge is not to prevent narrative warfare. That is impossible. The challenge is to participate consciously—knowing when to resist, when to reframe, and when to listen differently.

This chapter does not end with reassurance. It ends with responsibility. If stories shape reality, then the stories we tell—about ourselves, our enemies, our histories—must be chosen with the same seriousness as any act of diplomacy or defence. The next war may not be fought on land or sea, but in the spaces between what people believe and what they *need* to believe. *And that is the most strategic terrain of all.*

Economic Siege: Sanctions and Soft Wars

A war fought through economic levers can achieve what military aggression often cannot: prolonged pressure without open confrontation, systemic destabilisation without immediate casualties, and strategic victory without the spectacle of violence. Sanctions, embargoes, tariffs, and financial exclusions now function not as supporting mechanisms of diplomacy, but as autonomous instruments of coercion—*weapons of influence*, deliberately designed to reshape behaviour, fracture alliances, and weaken states. In the modern landscape, conflict often begins not with the roar of tanks, but with a silent freeze on bank accounts or a sudden cutoff from global trade. War, increasingly, comes dressed as bureaucracy.

The evolution of economic warfare reflects a broader shift in how power is wielded and how legitimacy is claimed. Traditional wars carry visibility and moral consequence. Economic wars are deniable, slow-moving, and largely immune from real-time scrutiny. This asymmetry makes them particularly attractive to states seeking strategic advantage without the political cost of kinetic engagement. A well-constructed sanctions regime can exert pressure on a regime's internal elite, suppress technological development, isolate a nation diplomatically, or fracture its social fabric through induced scarcity—all while the aggressor maintains the public posture of restraint. *Economic warfare is the art of inflicting suffering with plausible deniability.*

Consider the US-led sanctions against Iran, a campaign refined over decades and culminating in the so-called "maximum pressure" approach during the Trump administration. By targeting key sectors—oil exports, banking, metal industries—and cutting Iran off from the SWIFT international payments system, the United States effectively throttled the country's economic lifeline. The rial collapsed, inflation soared, and access to basic medicines became erratic. Yet the architects of these sanctions insisted that their goal was not to punish the people of Iran but to compel a policy shift on nuclear development. Here lies the conceptual tension: when a population suffers in order to exert leverage on its government, the line between targeted coercion and collective punishment becomes dangerously blurred.

The Soviet-era blueprint for economic siege was more infrastructural. During the Cold War, the United States and its allies used export controls under the Coordinating Committee for Multilateral Export Controls (CoCom) to prevent advanced Western technology from reaching the Eastern Bloc. These weren't traditional embargoes. They were more sophisticated—filters of knowledge, innovation, and industrial momentum. While the USSR could build rockets and tanks, it fell dramatically behind in microelectronics, computing, and automation—precisely the sectors the West cordoned off. The result wasn't immediate collapse but cumulative attrition. In this sense, the Cold War was not just a race for military dominance but an *economic contest disguised as an arms race.*

In the contemporary arena, economic coercion is no longer the sole province of the United States or its Western allies. China's economic statecraft now extends well beyond Belt and Road investments or debt diplomacy. Its selective application of trade bans—such as halting rare earth mineral exports to Japan in 2010 following maritime disputes—illustrates how Beijing deploys commerce as an assertion of sovereignty. More recently, Lithuania found itself economically blacklisted by China after allowing Taiwan to open a de facto embassy under its own name in Vilnius. Chinese customs reportedly began rejecting Lithuanian goods, pressuring EU-based companies to disassociate. This form of "silent embargo" avoids overt declarations, instead leveraging scale and ambiguity to intimidate. *The genius of soft economic warfare lies in its strategic subtlety—it punishes without proclamation.*

Critics argue that sanctions rarely achieve their stated political aims. Cuba, subjected to a near-total US embargo since 1960, remains under single-party rule. North Korea, under some of the harshest sanctions globally, has only doubled down on its nuclear ambitions. Yet to measure efficacy solely in regime change is to miss the wider effects. Sanctions signal international norms. They isolate violators. They freeze assets, complicate supply chains, and corrode the morale of governing elites. And sometimes, their success is not regime collapse but delay—postponing military modernisation, obstructing illicit finance, or limiting diplomatic mobility. *Economic war is often not about forcing surrender. It's about raising the cost of defiance beyond what the adversary is willing to pay.*

However, the humanitarian toll cannot be abstracted. When the United Nations imposed sanctions on Iraq in the 1990s, after Saddam Hussein's invasion of Kuwait, it led to widespread shortages of medicine and clean water. Some estimates attribute hundreds of thousands of child deaths to the resulting conditions. In retrospect, these sanctions became a cautionary tale: blunt economic pressure can delegitimise international law when it turns a civilian population into collateral. This legacy prompted reforms, such as the development of "smart sanctions," targeted at elites and specific entities. Yet even targeted sanctions can have unintended consequences—private companies withdraw beyond what is legally required, banks over-comply, and supply chains fracture, leading to broader social impact.

What makes modern economic warfare more complex than its historical antecedents is the interdependence of global markets. During the Cold War, the divide between capitalist and communist economies allowed for compartmentalised pressure. Today, nations trade with their adversaries. Russian gas warms European homes; American semiconductors power Chinese electronics; Taiwanese microchips sit in military hardware used by rival states. This interconnectedness makes economic sanctions both more potent and more perilous. The 2022 sanctions on Russia, following its invasion of Ukraine, triggered cascading disruptions in energy markets, food security, and commodity prices across the world. Sri Lanka's debt crisis, Egypt's inflation spiral, and Pakistan's fuel shortages were not directly targeted by sanctions—but they were downstream casualties of a war waged through pipelines and ports.

And yet, economic siege is not only a tool of states. Non-state actors, corporations, and even consumer collectives increasingly wield economic pressure to shape political outcomes. Boycotts, divestment campaigns, and shareholder activism represent a form of soft warfare internal to civil society. In some cases, they align with state interests. In others, they challenge them. For example, the BDS (Boycott, Divestment, Sanctions) movement targeting Israel's occupation policies has spurred both legislative crackdowns and global debate. Here, the tools of economic pressure mimic those of traditional sanctions—but with grassroots origin and moral framing. The boundaries between war and protest, between pressure and punishment, are no longer clearly demarcated.

Economic siege also plays out in digital space. In 2021, the Biden administration blacklisted a suite of Chinese tech companies citing surveillance abuses and national security concerns. The implications went beyond trade restrictions—they impacted global partnerships, investment patterns, and talent flows. Silicon Valley firms, wary of scrutiny, began unwinding relationships. Universities faced dilemmas over joint research. Venture capital reallocated. These decisions—appearing individually prudent—collectively reshaped entire technological ecosystems. *Economic war is now conducted through regulation, code, and capital allocation as much as through embargoes and tariffs.*

To make sense of this shifting terrain, one must understand that economic pressure is rarely about immediate results. It is a strategy of strategic patience, signalling, and attrition. Its success depends less on visible victories than on cumulative constraints. But this makes it ethically fraught. When does pressure become persecution? When does deterrence become collective punishment? And who decides when the war is "worth it"?

Strategic restraint requires a framework beyond utility. Economic weapons—like their military counterparts—must be governed by proportionality, intent, and accountability. Sanctions should be coupled with clear diplomatic pathways, humanitarian exceptions, and periodic review. Without these, they risk becoming moral theatre: expressive acts that satisfy domestic politics but inflict disproportionate harm abroad.

At its best, economic pressure can be a force for non-violent change. The sanctions against apartheid-era South Africa, for instance, played a significant role in delegitimising the regime internationally and supporting the internal anti-apartheid movement. But at its worst, economic siege calcifies authoritarianism, breeds black markets, and punishes the innocent to coerce the guilty. The difference lies not in the tool, but in the precision, purpose, and accountability of its use.

This subchapter does not offer prescriptions. It offers frameworks for discernment. As economic weapons proliferate, we must ask not only *whether* they work, but *how* they work, *on whom*, and *at what cost.* In an age where war may arrive through supply chains rather than armies, *strategic morality is no longer optional. It is infrastructure.*

Cultural Erasure and Identity Wars

Destroying a culture is never only about artefacts, rituals, or language. It is an assault on a people's sense of time—past, present, and future. To erase a culture is to dislocate a population from its historical coordinates, to rupture the continuity that makes identity durable and coherent. Unlike physical war, which kills bodies, *cultural war aims to kill memory.* This form of aggression is often more enduring and more insidious because it attacks what cannot be rebuilt: the silent agreements between generations, the metaphors that bind community, and the images that dignify a people's place in the world.

In March 2001, the Taliban reduced to rubble the Bamiyan Buddhas—two towering sixth-century statues carved into sandstone cliffs in central Afghanistan. These were not just religious icons; they were historical witnesses. For centuries, they had stood as emblems of the region's pre-Islamic past, of its position along the Silk Road, of its layered pluralism. Their demolition was not a product of strategic military logic. It was ideological. By destroying these statues, the Taliban aimed to signal dominance over the narrative of Afghan identity—to sever the thread between a diverse past and a homogenised present. *The goal was not to defeat an enemy but to extinguish an alternative memory.*

But cultural erasure is not always explosive or sudden. Far more often, it is methodical and disguised in the language of reform or civilisation. Colonial re-education projects throughout the nineteenth and twentieth centuries worked not by demolishing temples but by replacing them—substituting indigenous cosmologies with imported worldviews. In British India, missionary schools taught Indian children that their own traditions were irrational or inferior. In Canada and Australia, indigenous children were removed from their families under state-sanctioned assimilation policies, forced to unlearn their languages, their songs, and their names. The violence here was bureaucratised, yet no less devastating. Over time, the trauma compounded: generations grew up estranged from their cultural anchors, learning to see their inheritance as shame rather than strength.

This reveals an uncomfortable truth: *cultural erasure is often enacted not by fanatics, but by administrators.* It is designed not to terrorise, but to "improve." And it becomes especially potent when accompanied by legal, economic, and educational pressures that reward forgetting and penalise resistance. The metrics of success in these campaigns are not battlefield victories but shifts in language, dress, naming practices, and belief systems. Culture is not erased in a single event; it is overwritten, sometimes with the consent of the victim.

The twentieth century produced some of the most systematic efforts at cultural annihilation under the guise of national unity. During the Khmer Rouge's reign in Cambodia, intellectuals, artists, and monks were executed en masse as part of a campaign to eliminate not just dissent, but complexity. Language was flattened, traditional dress banned, and familial roles reorganised. This wasn't a purge of opposition—it was a war against ambiguity. Similarly, during China's Cultural Revolution, young Red Guards destroyed temples, ancestral tablets, and classical texts with the conviction that history itself had to be abolished to purify the nation. In both cases, the destruction of heritage was not a by-product of ideological fervour—it *was* the ideology. The past had to be razed for the future to be re-scripted.

What makes a civilisation resilient to such attacks is not its monuments or its manuscripts, but its ability to transmit meaning under pressure. Oral traditions, underground education, hidden rituals—all function as vessels of survival. The Jewish diaspora, particularly under Roman and later Christian persecution, preserved identity through portable texts and adaptive religious practices. Armenian communities, despite the Ottoman genocide and decades of Soviet cultural repression, used liturgy, music, and language as resistance tools. In both cases, resilience emerged not from the preservation of structures but from the preservation of *symbols*—the inner scaffolding of identity.

Yet, there is a critical distinction between cultural survival and cultural stagnation. A society's resilience is not merely about conserving the past but about reinterpreting it without surrendering its essence. When cultural identity becomes overly defensive—fixated on purity or frozen in nostalgia—it risks collapsing under the weight of external threats or internal dogma. The ability to *re-narrate* one's story in the face of dislocation is what differentiates durable cultures from fragile ones.

This brings us to the strategic utility of culture in modern geopolitics. While physical conquest may have become more difficult due to international law and multilateral alliances, *cultural influence remains a key vector of power.* The Chinese state's Confucius Institutes, the American export of pop culture, and Russia's deployment of historical revisionism through state media are all examples of soft power used to reframe national narratives both at home and abroad. These are not just exercises in public diplomacy; they are *pre-emptive memory wars*—attempts to shape how the next generation understands history, identity, and legitimacy.

But cultural imperialism is not solely the domain of great powers. Small nations, too, participate in these struggles by asserting their uniqueness and broadcasting it through art, film, and digital storytelling. Ukraine's resistance to Russian aggression has not been waged only with arms, but with images, anthems, and historical clarifications. The blue-and-yellow flag painted on bombed buildings, the viral folk songs on TikTok, and the insistence on using Ukrainian place names over Russian equivalents are all forms of *cultural counter-offensive.* They say: we exist not just politically, but symbolically.

The digital age has paradoxically amplified both the risk and the reach of cultural erasure. On one hand, online platforms can preserve endangered languages, archive oral histories, and connect diasporas. On the other, algorithms prioritise content that is legible to the global mainstream, often eroding linguistic and aesthetic diversity. When a billion people use the same visual templates, listen to the same sound loops, and scroll through the same curated feeds, *difference begins to dissolve.* This is not an intentional war on culture, but it is a war of *standardisation*—a quiet flattening of nuance under the logic of scale.

To counter this, resilience must be conscious. Cultures that survive are not those with the most resources, but those that *remember deliberately.* This means investing in intergenerational mentorship, in education that teaches not just skills but stories, in institutions that are humble enough to preserve and agile enough to adapt. Cultural identity is not a museum piece; it is a living strategy. And like any strategy, it must respond to changing threats without forfeiting its core.

The notion of cultural war challenges us to rethink what victory and loss look like. A nation may retain its borders and lose its soul. A people may survive demographic collapse yet transmit a worldview that persists in exile. The real question is not whether a culture can defend itself, but whether it can outlast attempts to be forgotten.

Ultimately, the erasure of culture is not about the absence of buildings or books. It is about the absence of continuity—of people who can explain not just *what* a tradition means, but *why* it matters. Civilisations endure not because they are powerful, but because they are meaningful. And when that meaning is threatened, the frontline is not drawn on maps. It is drawn in memory.

The Silent Wars We Inhabit

There are wars without armies, trenches, or treaties—fought not with bullets, but with self-doubt, distraction, and dislocation. These are the silent wars: battles of identity, meaning, purpose, and anxiety that play out within the minds of individuals rather than across maps of territory. They rarely make headlines, yet they are just as consequential. And for many, they are lifelong campaigns. In these conflicts, clarity is scarce, the enemy elusive, and the rules undefined. But here too, *the logic of warfare has something to teach us—not about how to destroy, but how to endure and rebuild.*

One of the most compelling paradoxes of wartime experience is that while it subjects individuals to chaos, it often produces a kind of psychological lucidity. Soldiers, aid workers, and survivors of war zones frequently speak of an acute awareness—of what matters, what doesn't, and who they are beneath their social armour. Stripped of routine comforts and thrown into states of existential urgency, they access something civilians often lack: *an unfiltered sense of purpose.* The stakes are visible, decisions matter, and distraction evaporates. Within horror, there is clarity.

This raises a provocative question: if war produces focus, can *less destructive forms of pressure* be used to help civilians attain similar psychological insights? And more pointedly—what if the frameworks developed in military strategy, decision science, and combat psychology offer valuable tools for navigating our own personal uncertainties?

Begin with the internal fragmentation so many experience today. The average modern individual is torn between competing roles—parent, professional, citizen, partner—and these identities often conflict rather than cohere. Social media intensifies this dissonance by projecting curated ideals while eroding private boundaries. Meanwhile, traditional anchors of meaning—religion, community, even geography—have weakened, leaving individuals to self-construct their identity from an ever-expanding menu of options. *Choice, once a symbol of freedom, has become a terrain of confusion.* What we face is not a crisis of morality or intelligence, but one of integration.

Like a commander overwhelmed by intelligence reports, we know too much and understand too little.

Wartime thinkers, from Sun Tzu to Clausewitz to modern defence planners, have long understood the value of *prioritisation under pressure*. In battle, information overload can kill. Successful strategy depends not on seeing everything, but on *knowing what to ignore*. This principle applies directly to modern civilian life. In a world of unlimited content, inputs, and choices, *clarity emerges from constraint*. Learning to identify what is strategically essential—rather than reactively urgent—is perhaps the most transferable lesson from wartime cognition. In psychological terms, this means cultivating *discipline of attention*: knowing which voices to heed, which conflicts to pursue, and which battles to forfeit.

Similarly, the challenge of anxiety can be reframed through the lens of readiness. Anxiety, in evolutionary terms, is a misdirected preparedness mechanism. It evolved to prime the body and mind for potential threat, but in contemporary society it has become chronic and contextless. In warfare, readiness is tied to *mission, not mood*. Soldiers are trained to prepare even in the absence of immediate danger. Likewise, civilian resilience grows when preparation replaces projection—when one replaces vague anticipatory dread with concrete contingency planning. Anxiety loses much of its grip when it is given *structure*. It becomes bearable when it is named, scoped, and managed like a tactical variable—not an existential verdict.

This is not to romanticise militarism, nor to suggest that human problems are best approached through martial metaphors. The aim is subtler: to extract *psychological frameworks* from wartime contexts and apply them to peacetime dilemmas. Take, for instance, the concept of a "fog of war"—the idea that no commander has perfect information, and must still act decisively. Civilian analogues are everywhere: the entrepreneur launching a product with incomplete data, the teacher adapting to a shifting classroom, the parent making choices under emotional strain. In all cases, moral and practical clarity emerge not from certainty, but from *the ability to act well despite uncertainty*. One does not wait for the fog to lift; one learns to move within it.

Moral ambiguity is another front on which internal wars are waged. Consider the individual trying to navigate professional ambition while staying true to ethical values. Or the citizen trying to discern truth in an ecosystem polluted by spin and polarisation. Wartime dilemmas—such as whether to follow questionable orders or protect civilians at risk to self—mirror these in structure if not in scale. One lesson from soldiers who have faced real ethical trauma is that *small choices compound.* The erosion of moral clarity does not happen all at once; it begins with rationalisation. Civilians often excuse moral drift as "realism" or "complexity," but war teaches that clarity is not the absence of complexity—it is the discipline of drawing lines in its midst.

And then there is the war of *purpose.* Perhaps the most silent and insidious battle of all. Without purpose, even comfort becomes hollow. Victor Frankl, in his reflections on surviving Nazi concentration camps, observed that those who survived longest were not the physically strongest, but those who maintained *a sense of meaning.* In peacetime, the absence of suffering does not guarantee peace of mind. It is often the lack of meaningful struggle—not its excess—that renders modern life unbearable. The proliferation of pseudo-conflicts—outrage cycles, digital feuds, invented drama—can be seen as compensations for the absence of *authentic stakes.* Individuals seek friction not because they want chaos, but because they are starved of *clarity.*

How, then, can wartime frameworks help restore peace? First, by encouraging intentional conflict. That is, recognising that some tensions are not to be avoided but *engaged consciously.* For example, identity conflict—am I a parent or a professional? Am I loyal to tradition or innovation?—can be paralysing until reframed as a strategic dilemma: which role serves the broader mission at this moment? The goal is not to suppress inner conflict but to *orchestrate it*, as a general coordinates divisions within a larger army.

Second, by cultivating a sense of mission. Mission need not be heroic. It can be modest but clear: to parent well, to mentor wisely, to build something that endures. A mission, like a wartime objective, *organises the chaos of daily decisions.* It offers not answers, but orientation. Even when outcomes are uncertain, one's *alignment* remains intact.

Lastly, by reclaiming agency in the face of disorder. Modern life teaches helplessness—systems are too big, institutions too opaque, the self too fragmented. War teaches the opposite lesson: *you may not control the field, but you control your posture on it.* That lesson is profoundly transferable. In every silent war—whether against addiction, grief, indecision, or despair—the first victory is reclaiming the ground of one's own will.

It would be a mistake to overstate the analogy between personal struggle and actual warfare. But it would also be a mistake to dismiss the parallels entirely. The architecture of conflict—fog, friction, fragmentation, decision under pressure—is universal. What changes is the terrain. And if war has taught humanity anything, it is that peace is not the default state. It is *engineered.* It is planned, defended, and negotiated, often against invisible adversaries within.

The final insight may be this: peace is not merely the absence of internal conflict, but the *integration of conflict into a meaningful framework.* The silent wars we inhabit do not need to be won in the traditional sense. They need to be *understood.* And from understanding comes not surrender, but *strategy*. Not silence, but *resolution.*

Chapter 10
What the Ashes Teach Us: Toward a Conscious Future

Some lessons creep upon us long after they are needed. Others, painfully forged, arrive exactly when our minds are prepared to receive them. War, stripped of its euphemisms and justifications, belongs squarely to the latter kind. It lays bare what political theory softens, what public rhetoric distorts, and what the solitary conscience cannot quite encompass: the extremes of human capacity—from barbarity to selflessness. The question is not merely how to halt such conflicts, but how to absorb the truths they force upon us. What becomes of the knowledge war grants us—about our character, our institutions, our cherished myths? What sort of civilisation can rise from ruins without falsifying its own foundations?

A difficult premise must be faced at the outset: the way we remember wars shapes the likelihood of their return. National memory is never a passive ledger; it is a form of instruction. Through stone memorials, ceremonial dates, school lessons, and the language of film, nations construct curated narratives of conflict. Omission is as instructive as inclusion—often more so. In many places, remembrance has drifted towards stylised pageantry, where banners and tales of gallantry smother the awkward realities of political folly, civilian agony, and moral compromise. To recall responsibly is to refuse both amnesia and embellishment. It calls for a balance—nuance without excuse, respect without theatrical piety.

Post-war Germany offers one model: an institutionalised reckoning with guilt, not as an act of self-flagellation but as a safeguard for its democracy. Set this against revisionist strands in parts of East Asia, the Balkans, and even in the United States, where selective nostalgia dulls the blade of self-examination. The core question is not whether a nation should take pride in sacrifice or survival. It is whether that pride can coexist with a searching critique of the policies and ideas that demanded such sacrifice in the first place. At its most honest, commemoration is less about closure than about recalibration—realigning the moral compass by refusing to tidy away the past.

From here emerges a subtler dilemma: how to prepare for the next war without hastening its arrival. Deterrence, the prevailing creed of the Cold War, thrived on paradox—avoiding conflict by standing ready to unleash it. Yet readiness can, with little warning, shade into hunger. Stockpiles and arsenals are marketed as prudence, but they reshape diplomatic posture, drain public coffers, and raise the stakes for any failure in negotiation. Is there a different kind of preparedness—anchored not in weapons, but in ethical foresight?

This is where the idea of *pre-emptive moral architecture* takes root. Just as engineers strengthen buildings against tremors, can we shape our institutions—and ourselves—to withstand moments of moral upheaval? This is no abstraction. It touches military training, the framing of humanitarian law, the selection of leaders, and the civic education of citizens. A society that rehearses its ethical limits in times of calm stands a far better chance of holding them in crisis. The aim is not moral flawlessness, but a kind of resilience that holds fast when the winds rise.

At the heart of this framework sits a virtue often dismissed as sentimental: hope. Military planners rarely count it among their assets; it is seen as too soft, too naïve. Yet history tells another tale. During the grimmest stretches of the Second World War, Allied cohesion was sustained partly by a shared vision—of liberation, of rebuilding, of a different world to follow. Hope served as a long-burning fuel, not because it promised victory, but because it gave shape and meaning to endurance. It is less about optimism than orientation—a way of facing forward, even when the present is nearly unbearable.

In our present century—fractured by polarisation, environmental peril, and the quiet manipulations of algorithms—cynicism often passes itself off as sophistication. Yet cynicism builds nothing. It can dismantle illusions, yes, but offers no scaffolding in their place. The future, if it is to be more than a recycling of the present, demands constructive imagination. Not escapist fantasy, but a vision rooted in the lessons of our darkest hours. And such vision must be woven into the very fabric of civic life—into the subjects taught to children, the laws drafted in parliament, the designs of our cities, the rituals we share. Without that, peace becomes merely an interlude between storms.

Perhaps war's most unsettling gift is the mirror it forces into our hands—not to humiliate, but to show, without distortion, what we defend, what we destroy, and what we overlook. Stripped of propaganda, war clarifies. It maps the fractures in our morality, the brittleness of our systems, the gaps in our own narratives. And it leaves us with a question most would rather leave unasked: if this is what we reveal under strain, what must we strengthen now, in stillness, to become something better?

No utopias will be offered here. What follows instead is a framework—a set of lenses—through which to see how remembrance, preparedness, vision, and moral architecture touch not only foreign policy and military thinking, but the design of neighbourhoods, the governance of the digital sphere, the texture of everyday life. The argument is simple enough: truly learning from war makes us less inclined to fight it, not more. It sharpens awareness—of power, of consequence, of possibility.

And so this book closes not by recoiling from war's shadows, but by meeting them with steady eyes. To learn from war is not to court violence; it is to study failure until it instructs. From the ash and debris comes a reminder both sobering and strangely hopeful: the future will not fall into our laps, nor will it arrive unshaped. It will be moulded—by what we have endured, by what we choose to build, and by the quiet, stubborn courage of those who remember enough to refuse repetition.

Remembering Without Glorifying

History is not only what happened. It is also what is remembered, and perhaps more critically, *how* it is remembered. War, with its staggering human cost and far-reaching consequences, occupies a central place in national memory. Yet remembrance is never neutral. It is shaped by the victors, curated by institutions, and passed down in classrooms, parades, memorials, and films. Every nation, knowingly or not, makes a choice: to remember with sobriety or to remember with splendour. The difference between the two can shape foreign policy, social cohesion, and even the ethical bearing of a people.

The act of commemorating war is always political. It functions not merely as a tribute to the past but as a script for the future. A society that remembers war primarily through medals and battlefield heroics tends to normalise sacrifice for the nation, often without questioning the policies or prejudices that brought it there. By contrast, remembrance that centres grief, civilian loss, and the ethical chaos of conflict is far more likely to inoculate a population against the seduction of future violence. *Remembrance, then, is not just about honour—it is about orientation.* And it is one of the most powerful tools a state possesses in shaping its civic identity.

Consider two post-war societies that adopted radically different approaches to memory: Germany and Japan. Following the Second World War, Germany instituted a policy of *Vergangenheitsbewältigung*—"coming to terms with the past"—that emphasised education, moral reckoning, and public shame over militarism. Holocaust memorials occupy prominent space in Berlin. Students are required to study the atrocities committed under the Nazi regime. Commemoration is laced with remorse, not pride. The result is a nation that, despite internal tensions, has largely succeeded in deterring neo-nationalism from entering mainstream legitimacy.

Japan, by contrast, pursued a policy of strategic ambiguity. While the Hiroshima Peace Memorial serves as a powerful symbol of nuclear devastation, much of the nation's wartime aggression—particularly in China and Korea—has been downplayed or omitted from textbooks. The controversial Yasukuni Shrine, which honours both regular soldiers and convicted war criminals, remains a flashpoint in East Asian geopolitics. Japan's remembrance practices, by focusing more on national victimhood than responsibility, have impeded regional reconciliation. Both examples make one thing clear: *how a nation frames its war memory directly influences its domestic values and international posture.*

The United States presents yet another case. From Arlington Cemetery to blockbuster films like *Saving Private Ryan*, the American narrative of war is dominated by themes of liberation, heroism, and moral clarity. Vietnam remains a partial exception—its ambiguous legacy has rendered it less cinematic and less celebrated. But in most other cases, military interventions are remembered in terms of noble intention and individual sacrifice. Rarely are the underlying political calculations, failed intelligence, or unintended consequences given equal moral weight. This creates a form of cultural myopia: a people deeply grateful to its veterans, but often incurious about the wars themselves. *To honour soldiers without scrutinising the wars they fought is to privilege sentiment over understanding.*

This tension is not unique to global powers. In Rwanda, the post-genocide government has carefully orchestrated a collective narrative that frames the Tutsi-led Rwandan Patriotic Front as liberators. While this has aided national unity and stability, it has also silenced dissent and buried crimes committed by the victors. In Turkey, the memory of the Armenian genocide remains officially unacknowledged—enshrined in denial rather than truth-telling. Meanwhile, in post-colonial nations, statues of imperial figures are increasingly challenged, not merely because they represent violent pasts, but because their continued presence signals unresolved power dynamics in the present. *Remembrance is never merely about the past; it is a living dialogue with the future.*

What, then, does it mean to remember without glorifying? It begins with complexity. Glorification thrives on simplification—clear villains, brave heroes, redemptive arcs. But war, by its nature, resists this narrative. Even just wars produce atrocities. Even honourable soldiers follow flawed commands. Remembering without glorifying means *resisting the urge to simplify for the sake of comfort.* It means confronting the ambiguity of motives, the grey areas of resistance and collaboration, and the enduring psychological toll on combatants and civilians alike.

It also requires institutional humility. Governments must allow space for critical voices—historians, artists, survivors—to challenge the official narrative. This includes funding for museums that foreground civilian experience, education policies that confront uncomfortable truths, and public spaces that prioritise mourning over spectacle. The Vietnam Veterans Memorial in Washington D.C., designed by Maya Lin, remains a powerful example. Its minimalist black granite wall, inscribed with names rather than political slogans, invites reflection rather than celebration. *It dignifies the dead without sanctifying the war.*

Technology adds a new dimension. In the digital age, memory is no longer controlled by states alone. Social media, online archives, and documentary platforms allow competing narratives to coexist and clash. This pluralism is both empowering and destabilising. It makes history less monolithic, but also more susceptible to misinformation and tribalism. The danger today is not that memory is too fixed—it is that it is too fragmented. Without shared frameworks for remembrance, societies risk falling into echo chambers of grievance, each convinced of its own righteousness. *Remembering responsibly in the 21st century thus requires both decentralisation and discernment.*

Importantly, remembrance without glorification is not anti-patriotic. It is, in fact, a higher form of patriotism—one that seeks not to romanticise the nation, but to mature it. It asks citizens to love their country enough to confront its failures. This is an uncomfortable task. But it is also an essential one, especially in democracies, where public opinion shapes policy and memory informs moral boundaries. *A mature patriotism does not require the denial of pain, but the integration of truth.*

In practical terms, this has several implications. First, it means rethinking how war anniversaries are observed. Beyond military parades and wreath-laying, such moments could be used for public forums, survivor testimonies, or debates about current foreign policy. Second, it calls for inclusive remembrance—acknowledging not just soldiers but also civilians, resisters, refugees, and even the so-called "enemy". Third, it suggests a long-term investment in historical literacy. Societies that understand their past with nuance are far better equipped to navigate present complexities.

There is also a personal dimension. Remembering without glorifying applies not only to nations but to individuals. Many veterans struggle with the dissonance between the public's romantic image of war and their own traumatic experience. Civilian populations, too, may inherit unexamined narratives from family, school, or media. To remember consciously is to *honour complexity over comfort, dignity over dogma.*

Ultimately, remembrance is an ethical act. It can harden or soften, vindicate or illuminate, isolate or connect. In the shadow of every war, we find a choice: to weaponise memory, or to humanise it. To mythologise conflict, or to learn from it. And perhaps this is the truest test of civilisation—not whether we can fight, but whether we can *remember* with enough depth, honesty, and empathy to avoid fighting again.

The Ethics of Preparedness

To prepare for war is, by conventional wisdom, to deter it. Yet history is littered with preparations that became provocations, defences that became triggers, and doctrines of readiness that escalated rather than restrained. The paradox is stark: *the better we prepare for violence, the more credible—and therefore tempting—its use becomes.* Beneath this tension lies a deeper moral challenge: can a society equip itself for potential conflict without, in the process, undermining the very peace it seeks to preserve? The answer depends less on weaponry and more on ethical architecture—what we might call *preemptive moral architecture.*

The idea of preemptive moral architecture begins with the recognition that preparation is not neutral. It is not simply the acquisition of capabilities, but the cultivation of intent. A bunker is never just concrete; it is an assumption about the world. A military drill is not just choreography; it is a rehearsal of ideology. From national budgets to foreign alliances, every act of "defence" encodes a worldview. That worldview can be cautious and sober, or it can be paranoiac and aggressive. Moral architecture, then, is not about whether a nation builds fences—it is about *how* it thinks about the neighbours beyond them.

Cold War history provides perhaps the clearest illustration of preparedness walking the line between deterrence and provocation.

The nuclear arms race between the United States and the Soviet Union was justified by both sides as a necessary hedge against annihilation. Each new deployment of missiles, each escalation in warhead yield, was presented as a rational act of precaution. But over time, these acts became indistinguishable from threats. By preparing to fight and survive nuclear war, both sides inadvertently made it more plausible. The Cuban Missile Crisis, arguably the closest the world has come to atomic war, was not a failure of deterrence—it was its logical endpoint. *When the theatre of preparation becomes so elaborate that it appears real, the line between simulation and conflict dissolves.*

This is not an argument against readiness per se. To be unprepared in the face of known threats is not pacifism; it is negligence. But ethical preparedness requires far more than physical tools. It demands an active interrogation of *what* is being prepared for, *why*, and under *what principles* conflict would ever be justified. In this context, preemptive moral architecture is the institutional, cultural, and philosophical scaffolding that constrains the misuse of readiness. It is the difference between defence as vigilance and defence as veiled aggression.

There are real-world frameworks that offer instructive parallels. The Geneva Conventions, for example, codify not just how war should be conducted but when it is ethically impermissible to fight. Their existence suggests that even in the ugliest domains of human behaviour, rules can shape conduct. But treaties are only as powerful as the moral cultures that uphold them. In Rwanda, Radio Télévision Libre des Mille Collines did not carry weapons, yet its broadcasts incited genocide. Preparedness in that case came not in the form of arms but in the creation of ideological momentum. *The most dangerous forms of preparation are not physical—they are narrative.*

Militaries themselves are not blind to this. Some of the most thoughtful doctrine writers today argue for the concept of "just readiness"—the idea that preparation should be bounded not only by operational need but by proportionality and intent. For example, the Norwegian Armed Forces have adopted training programmes that explicitly include ethical reasoning, cultural sensitivity, and laws of armed conflict as part of basic instruction. These are not aesthetic additions; they are *guardrails against the moral corrosion that unchecked preparedness can produce.*

This is especially relevant in the age of hybrid warfare, where traditional lines between peace and war have blurred. Cybersecurity drills, information warfare simulations, and artificial intelligence-based battlefield systems create a constant state of low-level mobilisation. The ethical question is no longer limited to *if* we go to war, but *how far we live within its logic even in peacetime.* If a society's infrastructure, economy, and consciousness are always postured for threat, does that not change its civic temperament, its foreign policy, its everyday anxieties?

Here is where preemptive moral architecture becomes critical. It is not about waiting for war and then invoking ethics—it is about *building the ethical constraints into the conditions of preparation itself.* This includes:

– Ensuring parliamentary oversight of defence budgets and acquisitions, so that preparation does not become the private domain of industrial lobbies.

– Embedding human rights and international law training at every level of military and civil service education.

– Encouraging public discourse around the psychological and political costs of "readiness" culture, including its impact on minority communities, dissent, and free speech.

– Developing diplomatic doctrines in tandem with defence doctrines, so that every investment in military capacity is matched by investment in conflict resolution capability.

In this sense, preemptive moral architecture is not a single policy but a posture—a long-term, deliberately cultivated ecosystem of restraint, reflection, and transparency. It is what ensures that when a drone is built, so is a doctrine for its ethical deployment. That when intelligence is gathered, so too is a system of accountability. *It is not anti-readiness. It is morally literate readiness.*

This concept also extends into personal and professional domains. Preparedness is not only national; it is psychological. People prepare for conflict every day—in boardrooms, classrooms, relationships. The ethical question remains: *can one prepare to assert oneself without escalating aggression?* In business, this might mean contingency planning that does not include character assassination. In leadership, it means building robust institutions without cultivating paranoia. The same principles apply: clarity of purpose, ethical transparency, and the refusal to let the possibility of conflict become a self-fulfilling prophecy.

One might counter: is it not naïve to moralise preparation in a world of ruthless actors? Shouldn't realism override idealism in national defence? The problem with this logic is that it assumes the two are opposed. But *the most enduring security comes not from supremacy but from credibility.* A nation that prepares with visible ethics—whose conduct is transparent, whose treaties are honoured, and whose readiness is grounded in public accountability—is more likely to attract allies and reduce threats than one that prepares through menace. Even adversaries recognise the difference between cautious strength and provocative posturing.

History punishes both extremes. Unchecked militarisation invites entanglements. Wilful unpreparedness invites exploitation. The task, then, is to cultivate a *middle ground that is not merely strategic, but moral.* This demands a new vocabulary—one that does not treat ethics as an afterthought to strategy, but as the architecture that makes strategy survivable in the long term.

Preemptive moral architecture challenges the common assumption that ethics and realism must always be at odds. In fact, the absence of ethical foresight often leads to strategic failure. Consider the 2003 invasion of Iraq. The military readiness was impeccable; the ethical preparedness was catastrophically deficient. Assumptions about welcome, stability, and legitimacy were drawn from a narrow, self-affirming worldview. The result was not only a human tragedy, but a strategic debacle that continues to shape global instability. *Preparation without ethical anchoring is not security—it is delusion.*

As technology amplifies the speed and scale of conflict—from autonomous weapons to deepfake propaganda—the urgency of ethical foresight increases. We may not be able to slow the pace of innovation, but we can design its use. Preemptive moral architecture is the blueprint that ensures tomorrow's tools do not undermine tomorrow's peace. And it begins today—not in war rooms, but in classrooms, legislatures, and public discourse.

Ultimately, preparedness is not just a technical state; it is a moral orientation. It is a statement about what a society believes is worth defending—and *how* it chooses to defend it. To prepare ethically is not to be naïve, but to be *clear-eyed enough to see that the habits of preparation are themselves political acts.* In a world where the weapons of war increasingly operate in shadows—cyber, narrative, financial—the ethics of preparedness may become the final frontier of human restraint. It will not be enough to arm ourselves with power. We must also arm ourselves with principle.

Hope as Strategy

To mention hope in the context of military planning often invites polite dismissal, if not outright disdain. It is too often relegated to the realm of sentiment—unquantifiable, untestable, and dangerously naïve in a world that prizes hard power and contingency logic. And yet, *history has repeatedly shown that hope—when rightly understood—is not the absence of realism, but the force that sustains it under the weight of chaos.* Hope is not the opposite of strategy; it is what makes long-term strategy possible.

At its most potent, hope is not optimism. It does not promise that things will go well. It does not rely on favourable odds. It is the decision to commit to outcomes that may seem impossible at present—but are morally necessary nonetheless. In this sense, hope is not about *expectation*, but about *orientation.* It governs what kind of future we aim for and whether we believe agency still matters, even when control has been stripped away. In war, as in life, there are moments where planning yields to uncertainty. *Hope is the discipline that ensures we still act with purpose even when clarity dissolves.*

Consider Václav Havel, the dissident playwright who became president of a free Czech Republic. In the darkest days of communist repression, Havel wrote about what he called "hope beyond outcomes"—a commitment to live as if truth mattered, even when lies prevailed. He was not a general. He did not command armies. But his vision shaped the moral terrain on which resistance gained momentum. Havel's hope was not a doctrine of passivity. It was the long-range fuel of civil courage.

The military historian John Keegan once argued that the most dangerous assumption in strategic thinking is that force alone can produce lasting political results. The most technically successful operations—whether Blitzkrieg or Shock and Awe—often fail when they ignore what people are fighting *for.* The United States' experience in Iraq is illustrative. Superior firepower and control of territory did not translate into stability, because strategic objectives lacked emotional resonance for the civilian population. *Hope was absent not just from the streets, but from the vision itself.*

This absence is not accidental. Strategic communities are taught to mistrust emotion, and understandably so. Emotional decision-making can cloud judgement. But *to strip emotion entirely from strategic frameworks is to make them brittle and short-sighted.* When leaders and institutions deny the role of hope, they often mistake pessimism for prudence and cynicism for intelligence. The result is a self-perpetuating logic of conflict management, rather than a vision for peace creation.

Strategic hope is different from fantasy. It does not ignore threats—it contextualises them. Nelson Mandela emerged from 27 years in prison to lead one of the most fragile transitions in modern political history. Had Mandela relied solely on legal restitution or demographic advantage, the country could have spiralled into civil war. Instead, he centred reconciliation—a hope-based strategy grounded in *the deliberate moral choice to prevent revenge.* It was not a gamble; it was a principled risk. And it worked because it was made visible, audacious, and structured into political life.

Hope, then, must be cultivated like any other capability. This demands systems, not slogans. Peace processes that succeed are those where hope is built into the architecture: mechanisms for inclusion, symbolic gestures that restore dignity, policies that reward cooperation rather than just penalise defection. The Good Friday Agreement, while far from perfect, codified hope into shared governance—not merely as an ideal, but as an operational strategy. *Without that structured hope, even ceasefires are fragile.*

In military planning, hope is often sidelined in favour of scenario modelling, game theory, and deterrence calculus. These tools are indispensable. But they describe what adversaries *might* do—not what societies *ought* to become. Strategic planning that lacks a hopeful telos tends to become reactive, trapped in short cycles of threat anticipation. This is how empires fall—not from loss of capacity, but from a corrosion of vision.

That corrosion often begins with language. Bureaucracies replace purpose with jargon. Wars are fought not for peace, but for "stability," "interests," or "strategic ambiguity." The more we abstract conflict from its human stakes, the more we weaken public resolve, international trust, and moral legitimacy. Hope, properly integrated, restores specificity. It insists on remembering what peace is for—not just what war is against.

Hope also changes how institutions behave under pressure. During the Second World War, Britain's decision to maintain cultural institutions, from the BBC to the National Gallery, was not decorative. It was strategic. Churchill reportedly refused to cut arts funding, saying, "Then what are we fighting for?" That line, apocryphal or not, captures the point: *in the worst of times, symbolic commitments to civilisation become acts of defiance.* To uphold beauty, truth, and education in war is to remind both allies and enemies that the conflict has a moral purpose worth enduring for.

In contemporary security contexts, the challenge is how to apply hope strategically without appearing naïve or unguarded. This is particularly relevant in counter-terrorism, where militarised responses often reinforce the narratives of grievance they aim to extinguish. A hope-centred approach would prioritise legitimacy over domination, emphasising justice, economic inclusion, and long-term political engagement. It is slower, less dramatic—but *it builds something the adversary cannot destroy: trust in institutions.*

This concept has important applications beyond formal warfare. In diplomacy, hope means imagining terms of engagement that transcend zero-sum thinking. In climate policy, it means investing in global cooperation not just as mitigation, but as intergenerational stewardship. In leadership, it means framing crises not as endpoints but as inflection points. Barack Obama's 2008 campaign was often mocked for its rhetorical emphasis on hope. But it reoriented political imagination, however briefly, and reminded citizens that change requires belief before it becomes policy. *Hope is not a platform; it is the soil from which all sustainable platforms grow.*

To be strategic about hope, then, is to make it credible, visible, and institutional. This requires:

– Framing public discourse around vision, not just defence

– Including social resilience and civic education in national security planning

– Funding peacebuilding, cultural diplomacy, and conflict prevention as seriously as kinetic capabilities

– Holding leaders accountable not only for results, but for the futures they invite citizens to imagine

In this framing, hope becomes a form of resistance—*resistance to fatalism, to strategic myopia, to the assumption that violence is inevitable and peace accidental.* To hope under oppression, to hope in a siege, to hope after atrocity—is not escapism. It is a strategic act of refusal to let the worst of human behaviour set the limits of what is politically possible.

Of course, hope alone is not enough. It must be married to competence, realism, and institutional rigour. But those who treat hope as mere ornament miss its operational value. It sustains morale.

It bridges polarisation. It legitimises compromise. *And it gives strategy a future worth surviving for.*

Perhaps the real test of a civilisation is not whether it can win wars, but whether it can imagine life beyond them. The most courageous generals, diplomats, and civic leaders in history were not those who mastered firepower, but those who *could still picture a horizon past the smoke.* Hope, when properly directed, is the compass that makes that imagination strategic. And in times when despair feels inevitable, *the decision to hope becomes the most disciplined act of leadership available.*

War's Final Gift

There is a dangerous seduction in war's drama: its banners, its heroes, its decisive moments. Much of history has been written under the influence of this allure—glorifying conquest, sanitising brutality, or reducing entire generations to chess pieces in strategic memoirs. Yet the most profound contribution war offers civilisation is not found in the myths it spawns but in the brutal clarity it forces. *War is not noble, but it is revealing.* And if we are prepared to face what it shows us—not just about states and armies, but about ourselves—we may come away with something rarer than victory: the capacity to choose differently next time.

When we strip away the abstractions of policy and patriotism, war becomes an intensely human theatre of decision-making under duress. Every conflict peels back the layers of ideology and custom to expose the primal, often contradictory drivers of human behaviour—fear, loyalty, vengeance, compassion, pride. These are not just battlefield phenomena; they are civilisational truths laid bare. *War clarifies what peacetime obscures.* In moments of threat and disintegration, we witness what people are truly willing to fight for, die for, betray for—or protect despite all odds.

What makes this clarity a gift, if anything, is that it is earned at extraordinary cost. Those who have truly seen war—the dismembered bodies, the impossible moral dilemmas, the slow grinding erosion of empathy—do not emerge inspired. They emerge changed. And if they speak honestly, they carry a moral urgency few civilians understand. Elie Wiesel once warned that the opposite of love is not hate but indifference. *War destroys not only bodies, but the inner architecture of care itself.* To study war responsibly, then, is to learn how to rebuild that architecture, brick by brick.

The most transformative military memoirs are not paeans to courage. They are reflections on ambiguity. Consider Karl Marlantes, a decorated Marine officer in Vietnam. His writing, particularly in *What It Is Like to Go to War*, is an unflinching account of the psychic dislocation that follows morally complex combat. Marlantes does not offer tidy lessons. Instead, he asks the reader to sit with war's contradictions—how one can act with honour in a context devoid of moral coherence, or how adrenaline can fuse with guilt in a permanent neural scar. His point is not that war is inherently evil. It is that *any experience that strips away illusion must be approached with ritual and reflection*—or it becomes toxic.

In this sense, war's "final gift" is not a gift at all unless it is received deliberately. It must be unpacked, studied, internalised, and then transmuted into civic, moral, or philosophical insight. Otherwise, the suffering remains unredeemed—just more broken bodies in the archive of human violence. The Nuremberg Trials, for instance, were not merely punitive. They were pedagogical. They insisted that even in the aftermath of industrial-scale atrocity, it was possible to articulate a moral framework for accountability. *This was not an act of vengeance; it was the beginning of post-war conscience.*

That conscience, however, is fragile. As public memory of war recedes, as veterans die, and as conflict becomes ever more technologised, the clarity war provides can easily be lost. We risk mistaking simulacra for substance—video game heroics for real human stakes, rhetorical battles for genuine moral complexity. The danger is not just forgetting, but *misremembering*: sentimentalising sacrifice without interrogating why it was required in the first place.

The post-9/11 era offers a cautionary example. The swift collapse of public discourse into binaries—freedom vs. terror, us vs. them—did more to undermine democratic vigilance than any terrorist plot could. It became easier to invoke courage than to examine causality. Yet those who returned from Iraq and Afghanistan did not return with tales of triumph. They returned with questions: about policy incoherence, civilian cost, moral dissonance, and the deep unease of applying tactical solutions to strategic voids. If war offers us a mirror, *it must be the kind we dare not look into only to reassure ourselves.*

The metaphor of the mirror is not used here lightly. It is perhaps the most apt image for what war reflects back at us: not a new identity, but the one we already carry—under stress, under threat, unmasked. Do we fight cleanly or cruelly? Do we protect the vulnerable or rationalise their sacrifice? Do we seek victory or vindication? These are not questions unique to generals. They are questions for citizens, legislators, teachers, and parents. *War is not only the failure of diplomacy; it is the stress test of values.*

One reason war continues to hold cultural fascination is that it offers something rare in modern life: heightened moral stakes. In combat, decisions are final. There is no corporate backroom or committee deferral. Choices made in seconds echo across generations. This gravity can intoxicate, but it can also teach. *If we are wise, we take that sense of gravity and bring it home—to boardrooms, classrooms, and family dinner tables.* The discipline of weighing cost, consequence, and ethical integrity should not be reserved for battlefield commanders. It is the work of any serious life.

Some of the most important lessons war offers are not about strategy but about restraint. The Cold War was not, in the end, won through missiles but through patience, containment, diplomacy, and cultural confidence. In that half-century standoff, restraint became the most courageous act of all. To not retaliate. To not overreach. To not collapse into panic. These are not signs of weakness. *They are signs that a nation has learned how to hold its power responsibly.* The fact that nuclear weapons have not been used in combat since 1945 is not a technological outcome; it is a moral achievement—however tentative.

Ultimately, what war teaches us is that every society is only as ethical as its behaviour under existential stress. This is when the real contours of a culture emerge—not during festivals or elections, but when the world turns volatile and uncertain. That is why remembrance matters—not to sanctify the past, but to discipline the present. Memorials and museums, if constructed well, do not glorify; they *warn.* They say: this was the edge of the abyss. You may get here again. Are you ready to act differently?

The final gift of war is not closure. It is accountability. It asks not how we celebrate heroes, but how we build systems that require fewer of them. It asks not whether a nation is willing to fight, but whether it is able to listen to the stories of those who did—and change accordingly. War does not ennoble us. *But it can awaken us—if we are brave enough to look at it without flinching, and humble enough to learn.*

In that learning, there is perhaps one hope that does not deceive: that the mirror war holds up might help us recognise what kind of people we wish to be—and what sacrifices we must avoid if we truly understand their cost. Not all knowledge is kind. But the knowledge war imparts, if received with conscience and courage, is the kind that prepares us not to repeat its worst offerings. And that, above all, may be the most enduring form of peace we can achieve.

About the Author

Alexander Carter Grey is a multidisciplinary historian and strategic psychologist who probes the hidden fault lines of human conflict. Long fascinated by how wars rewire minds, societies, and systems, Grey earned his PhD in Cognitive-Warfare Studies and has written widely in academic and mainstream journals on topics ranging from moral injury to crisis-led innovation. His work seamlessly integrates moral philosophy, cultural anthropology, and systems theory, and his distinctive narrative voice blends rigorous scholarship with evocative storytelling. With Wars That Changed the World, Grey invites readers to move beyond traditional military history and explore war as a crucible of transformation—psychologically, culturally, and philosophically—offering insights that resonate far beyond the battlefield.

www.ingramcontent.com/pod-product-compliance
Lightning Source LLC
Chambersburg PA
CBHW031345230926
51848CB00002B/394